Pillsbury

fast & healthy
cookbook

Delicious family meals in 30 minutes or less

WILEY
Wiley Publishing, Inc.

General Mills

Editorial Director: Jeff Nowak

Manager, Cookbooks: Lois Tlusty

Senior Health Editor:
Cheri Olerud

Senior Food Editor: Lola Whalen

Recipe Development and
Testing: Pillsbury Kitchens

Photography: General Mills
Photography Studios and Image
Library

Wiley Publishing, Inc.

Publisher: Natalie Chapman

Executive Editor: Anne Ficklen

Editor: Adam Kowit

Production Manager:
Michael Olivo

Senior Production Editor:
Jacqueline Beach

Cover Design: Suzanne Sunwoo

Art Director: Tai Blanche

Layout: Elizabeth Brooks,
Erin Zeltner

Manufacturing Manager:
Kevin Watt

Home of the Pillsbury Bake-Off® Contest

Pillsbury

For more great recipes
visit **pillsbury.com**

This book is printed on acid-free paper. ∞

For general information on our other products and services or for technical support, please contact our Customer Care Department within the United States at (800) 762-2974, outside the United States at (317) 572-3993 or fax (317) 572-4002.

Wiley also publishes its books in a variety of electronic formats. Some content that appears in print may not be available in electronic books. For more information about Wiley products, visit our web site at www.wiley.com.

Library of Congress Cataloging-in-Publication Data:

Pillsbury fast & healthy cookbook / Pillsbury editors.
    p.cm.
  Includes index.
  ISBN 978-0-470-28744-6 (paper : alk. paper)
 1. Quick and easy cookery. 2. Low-fat diet—Recipes. 3. Low-calorie diet—Recipes. 4. High-fiber diet—Recipes. I. Pillsbury Company. II. Title: Pillsbury fast and healthy cookbook.
  TX833.5.P548 2009
  641.5'55—dc22

2008019009

Printed in China

10 9 8 7 6 5 4 3

Cover photo: Grilled Marinated Shrimp, page 168

Yellow tomato, page 3 ©Stockdisc; Milk and eggs, page 8 ©PhotoDisc, Inc.; Cabbage, page 8 ©Stockdisc; Yellow tomato, page 8 ©Stockdisc; Watermelon, page 8 ©Stockdisc; Bread, page 8 ©Digital Vision; Cucumber, page 21 ©Stockdisc; Rice, page 47 ©PhotoDisc, Inc.; Carrot, page 71 ©PhotoDisc, Inc.; Onion, page 71 ©Stockdisc; Apple, page 146 ©Stockdisc

dear friends,

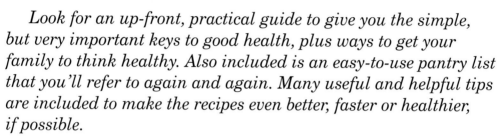

Great-tasting and healthy? Quick, too? All in one?

Surprisingly, you can get all three in one: great taste, health and fast recipes all come together in this new Pillsbury Fast & Healthy Cookbook.

Look for an up-front, practical guide to give you the simple, but very important keys to good health, plus ways to get your family to think healthy. Also included is an easy-to-use pantry list that you'll refer to again and again. Many useful and helpful tips are included to make the recipes even better, faster or healthier, if possible.

All 140 recipes follow the principles of healthy eating, being lower in fat and calories and higher in fiber and nutrients than most recipes. You can make any recipe in just three or four steps and all are done in 30 minutes or less, with Superfast recipes ready in 20 minutes or less.

Plan a memorable potluck recipe from the Fast Family Favorites chapter, make your next weeknight meal from the Meals in 20 Minutes Max chapter or pick an easy appetizer from the Fast and Fun Snacks chapter.

From Hot off the Grill to Skillet Meals and Casseroles to Sweet Treats, this book is a must-have for busy families.

Sincerely,
the Pillsbury editors

contents

fast and healthy lifestyle

Many of us want to lead healthier lives, whether just to feel better or to drop a few pounds. But with the fast pace of life, getting started can be a challenge. Here are some ways to begin.

eat dinner together

If your family eats dinner together most evenings, you already have a solid foundation and are well on your way to healthy eating. Research shows that families who eat together consume more fruits and vegetables, fiber, vitamins and minerals and less fat. The dinner table shapes good eating habits and homemade meals tend to be more wholesome with less added fat than take-out or restaurant foods. And, when families eat together, healthy eating is often a topic of conversation and the lessons learned can have a lasting impact.

find fast and healthy recipes

The recipes in this cookbook are perfect for time-pressed families—they taste great, are fast and easy and use everyday ingredients. They also:

- **contain** fruits, vegetables, beans and whole grains with fiber, vitamins A and C, calcium and iron

- **call** for canola and olive oils that are heart-healthy and good fats for stir-frying and cooking

- **use** fat-free (skim) milk, reduced-fat cheese and reduced-fat or fat-free cream cheese and sour cream

- **take** 10 to 30 minutes to prepare

- **list** calories, calories from fat, fat, saturated fat, trans fat, cholesterol, sodium, carbohydrate, dietary fiber and % Daily Value for vitamins A and iron and calcium per serving

5 steps to easy and healthy eating

These five actions are key to good health:

1. **Eat More Fruits and Vegetables:** Eating at least five servings of fruits and vegetables every day ensures that you get enough vitamins A and C and folic acid and other nutrients necessary for a healthy body.

2. **Choose Whole Grains and Foods High in Fiber:** Eating whole grains helps protect against heart disease, diabetes and certain cancers. Fiber keeps foods moving through your digestive tract. To increase your fiber, eat more beans and bran, and look for foods that contain at least three grams of fiber per serving. Equally important, when you increase the amount of fiber you eat, also increase the amount of water you drink, at least six to eight cups every day.

3. **Eat Foods Moderate in Fat and Cholesterol:** Reducing fat, especially saturated fat and cholesterol, matters. Replacing high-fat meats with lean cuts and low-fat substitutes, like using turkey kielbasa instead of pork kielbasa or using sirloin steak instead of stew meat, makes a big difference in lowering fat. Use canola or olive oil instead of butter or margarine for stir-fry and skillet dishes. Eat more beans and legumes, and less meat.

4. **Prepare Foods with Less Salt and Sugar:** Find ways to cut down on salt (sodium) and sugar. Omit salt from the cooking water when cooking pasta and rice. Eat less chips and crackers. Canned beans and vegetables are convenient and nutritious but contain sodium, so rinse them to reduce the sodium. To reduce sugar, eat less candy and baked goods like cake, doughnuts and muffins, and drink less soda pop.

5. **Be Active Every Day:** Devote 30 to 60 minutes most days on any activity you enjoy: walking, running, swimming, biking or whatever you choose. Being active helps prevent disease and maintain weight, builds healthy muscles, joints and bones, and promotes positive mental health and good sleeping habits. It's okay to break the time into smaller time segments—that's still beneficial for your heart and other muscles. It's important for the kids to be active, too. Go for a walk after dinner, play a game of tag, kick the soccer ball, toss the football or find other ways to encourage activity.

in your kitchen

You can make a big difference in reducing fat, sodium, cholesterol and calories when you select and cook fresh, healthy foods. Here's how:

- Cut down on the total amount of fat and saturated fat. When you use fat, think liquid and use canola or olive oil rather than solid butter, shortening or margarine.

- Cook without adding fat—braise, steam, poach or bake. Grilling, broiling and using a table-top grill are also good methods because they allow fat to drip off.

- Read food labels to compare sodium levels. Pick no-salt-added or low-sodium broths and other foods when you'd like to cut back. Don't add salt at the table, and don't cook potatoes, pasta or rice in salted water.

- Season the foods you prepare with herbs, lemon juice, vinegar, chopped fresh or dried herbs, chopped fresh chiles, sautéed chopped onions, garlic, gingerroot, spices and juices instead of salt.

- Boost the amount of potassium you eat to balance out the sodium. Eat foods that deliver potassium, including bananas, peaches, tuna, beans, spinach and tomatoes.

- If you'd like to reduce cholesterol, you can use egg whites and egg substitutes instead of whole eggs. Also increase cholesterol-lowering foods, like oats, barley and other grains.

- Select the most colorful fruits and vegetables, highest in vitamins, minerals and phytonutrients. Use frozen and canned fruits and vegetables, they're just as nutritious as their fresh counterparts. Add vegetables to stir-fries, soups and salads. Eat fruit as a snack or dessert, alone, paired with cheese or prepared in a recipe.

- Eat whole-grain breads and cereals made with oats, wheat, rice, corn and other grains. Add grains, legumes and beans to soups, stews and stir-fries to increase fiber and add texture.

fast and healthy family dinners pantry

Having the right ingredients on hand offers a lot of flexibility to prepare fresh, easy and great-tasting low-calorie, low-fat recipes. This pantry list covers the basics, with room to add your family's favorites.

Fresh Produce

Any fruit or vegetable in season

Broccoli

Cabbage

Carrots

Cucumbers

Garlic

Onions

Potatoes

Salad greens (any variety)

Spinach and other leafy greens

Sweet potatoes

Apples

Bananas

Grapes

Melons

Oranges, tangerines, grapefruit

Dairy

Fat-free (skim) or low-fat (1%) milk

Fat-free sour cream

Plain fat-free yogurt

Flavored fat-free yogurt

Squeeze or tub margarine for spreading

Light cream cheese

Low-fat or reduced-fat cheese

Meats/Poultry/Fish

Well-trimmed beef, pork and lamb cuts (e.g., "loin")

Skinless chicken and turkey

All types of shellfish and fish, especially fatty types, like salmon and tuna

Lean cold cuts (e.g., sliced roast turkey or beef)

Low-fat sausages (turkey)

Cereals/Pastas

Whole-grain cereals

Old-fashioned oatmeal

Whole-grain pasta, whole wheat couscous

Quinoa, bulgur wheat, quick-cook barley/other whole grains

Snacks

Whole-grain crackers or flatbreads

Rice crackers

Whole-wheat pretzels

Plain popcorn or low-fat microwave popcorn

Fig bars

Graham crackers

Canned and Bottled Goods

Reduced-sodium broths

Reduced-sodium tomato soup

Canned beans

Canned no-salt-added tomatoes

Fat-free bean dip

Canned fruits (in water or fruit juice)

Oils and Dressings/Sauces

Canola oil or soybean oil

Olive oil

Peanut butter

Low-fat or fat-free salad dressings

Sherry vinegar, balsamic vinegar and/or flavored vinegars

Pasta sauce

Salsa

Frozen Foods

Soy burgers and crumbles (look for low-fat brands)

Frozen juices: cranberry, orange, apple

Low-fat frozen yogurt

Whole-fruit freezer pops

Bakery

Whole-grain breads and rolls

Whole-grain English muffins

Whole-grain pitas

Corn tortillas

Whole wheat or white flour tortillas

Beverages

Flavored sparkling water

100% fruit juices

fast & fun snacks

chapter

1

Crispy Shrimp Tarts, see page 32

Frosty Mocha

 **Superfast**

Prep Time: 10 Minutes
Start to Finish:
10 Minutes
4 servings (1 cup each)

1½ cups fat-free (skim) milk

⅓ cup chocolate-flavor syrup

2 tablespoons natural-flavor malted milk powder, if desired

2 tablespoons instant coffee granules or crystals

3½ cups small ice cubes

1   In blender, place all ingredients except ice. Cover; blend on medium speed until well mixed.

2   Add ice cubes a few at a time, blending well on medium speed after each addition until smooth.

3   Pour into 4 glasses. Serve immediately.

1 Serving: Calories 110 (Calories from Fat 0); Total Fat 0g (Saturated Fat 0g; Trans Fat 0g); Cholesterol 0mg; Sodium 60mg; Total Carbohydrate 23g (Dietary Fiber 0g) **% Daily Value:** Vitamin A 4%; Vitamin C 0%; Calcium 10%; Iron 4% **Exchanges:** 1 Starch, ½ Other Carbohydrate **Carbohydrate Choices:** 1½

- Instant cappuccino coffee mix can be used in place of the regular coffee.

- To make chocolate shavings for a garnish, pull a vegetable peeler along the edge of a chocolate bar.

Ginger Tea Coolers

Prep Time: 25 Minutes

Start to Finish:
25 Minutes

6 servings (1 cup each)

3 cups water

1 piece (2 inches) unpeeled
fresh gingerroot, finely
chopped (2 tablespoons)

⅓ cup sugar

3 tea bags green tea or
3 teaspoons loose green tea

2 cups lime sparkling water

2 cups ice cubes

1 lemon, thinly sliced,
if desired

1 lime, thinly sliced, if desired

1 orange, thinly sliced,
if desired

1 In 2-quart saucepan, heat water, gingerroot and sugar to boiling over high heat, stirring to dissolve sugar. Reduce heat. Cover; simmer 5 minutes. Add tea bags; remove from heat. Cover; let steep 5 minutes.

2 Remove tea bags. Cool tea to room temperature, about 10 minutes. Pour through strainer into clean 2-quart pitcher.

3 Add sparkling water to pitcher. Fill 6 glasses with ice cubes. Pour mixture over ice cubes in glasses. Garnish with fruit slices.

1 Serving: Calories 50 (Calories from Fat 0); Total Fat 0g (Saturated Fat 0g; Trans Fat 0g); Cholesterol 0mg; Sodium 0mg; Total Carbohydrate 12g (Dietary Fiber 0g) **% Daily Value:** Vitamin A 0%; Vitamin C 0%; Calcium 0%; Iron 0% **Exchanges:** 1 Other Carbohydrate **Carbohydrate Choices:** 1

- Green tea is rich in heart-healthy antioxidants.

- Make extra tea "base" (through step 2) and keep refrigerated up to a week. Just add ice and sparkling water for refreshing iced tea anytime.

Peach-Berry Smoothie  Superfast

Prep Time: 5 Minutes
Start to Finish: 5 Minutes
4 servings (1 cup each)

2 containers (6 oz each) strawberry low-fat yogurt

1 cup sliced fresh or frozen peaches or nectarines

1 cup sliced fresh strawberries

1 cup crushed ice

1 In blender, place all ingredients. Cover; blend on high speed 30 to 60 seconds or until smooth.

2 Pour into 4 glasses. Serve immediately.

1 Serving: Calories 110 (Calories from Fat 10); Total Fat 1.5g (Saturated Fat 0.5g; Trans Fat 0g); Cholesterol 0mg; Sodium 55mg; Total Carbohydrate 19g (Dietary Fiber 1g) **% Daily Value:** Vitamin A 4%; Vitamin C 45%; Calcium 15%; Iron 0% **Exchanges:** ½ Fruit, ½ Other Carbohydrate, ½ Skim Milk **Carbohydrate Choices:** 1

how snacks stack up

SNACK	CALORIES	FAT
Corn chips (1 oz)	160	10g
Melba rounds (5)	50	0g
Potato chips, regular (1 oz)	150	10g
Potato chips, baked (1 oz)	110	1.5g
Pretzels (1 oz)	110	0g
Rice cake (1 cake)	35	0g
Round buttery crackers (5)	80	4g
Saltine crackers (5)	60	1.5g
Tortilla chips, regular (1 oz)	130	6g
Tortilla chips, baked (1 oz)	110	1g
Whole wheat crackers (7)	140	5g

Source: *USDA Handbook 8* and package labels

Serve this energizing fruit shake as a quick breakfast or as an after-school snack.

Frozen whole strawberries, slightly thawed, can be substituted for the fresh.

Very Berry Iced Tea

 **Superfast**

Prep Time: 10 Minutes

Start to Finish: 10 Minutes

8 servings (1 cup each)

4 cups water

3 tablespoons instant iced tea mix

3 cups raspberry-kiwifruit juice, chilled

½ cup fresh raspberries

1 In 2-quart pitcher, mix all ingredients except raspberries. Stir in raspberries.

2 Serve tea over ice in glasses.

1 Serving: Calories 60 (Calories from Fat 0); Total Fat 0g (Saturated Fat 0g; Trans Fat 0g); Cholesterol 0mg; Sodium 5mg; Total Carbohydrate 16g (Dietary Fiber 0g) **% Daily Value:** Vitamin A 0%; Vitamin C 10%; Calcium 0%; Iron 2% **Exchanges:** 1 Other Carbohydrate **Carbohydrate Choices:** 1

- For a special touch, freeze fresh raspberries in ice cubes and use them in glasses for this tea.

- Garnish with a small skewer of fresh kiwifruit pieces.

Strawberry-Orange Fruit Dip  Superfast

Prep Time: 15 Minutes

Start to Finish:
15 Minutes

12 servings dip (2 tablespoons each) and fruit

1 package (8 oz) ⅓-less-fat cream cheese (Neufchâtel), softened

¼ cup powdered sugar

½ teaspoon grated orange peel

½ cup chopped strawberries (about 3 oz)

Assorted fruit for dipping (12 whole strawberries, 2 kiwifruit, peeled and sliced, 12 pineapple chunks, 12 cantaloupe cubes)

1 In small bowl, beat cream cheese, powdered sugar and orange peel with electric mixer on low speed until smooth. Stir in chopped strawberries.

2 Serve with assorted fruit. Cover and refrigerate any remaining dip.

1 Serving: Calories 90 (Calories from Fat 40); Total Fat 4.5g (Saturated Fat 3g; Trans Fat 0g); Cholesterol 15mg; Sodium 80mg; Total Carbohydrate 9g (Dietary Fiber 1g) **% Daily Value:** Vitamin A 15%; Vitamin C 50%; Calcium 2%; Iron 0% **Exchanges:** ½ Fruit, ½ High-Fat Meat **Carbohydrate Choices:** ½

Use a microplane grater to remove just the orange part of the peel; the white pith underneath has a bitter taste.

You can make this dip up to one hour ahead. If you want to make it up to 24 hours ahead, stir in the chopped strawberries just before serving.

Mango-Mint Fruit Dip

 **Superfast**

Prep Time: 10 Minutes

Start to Finish:
10 Minutes

**16 servings (about
2 tablespoons dip and
⅔ cup fruit each)**

**1 cup chopped seeded peeled
mango (about ½ medium)**

**1 teaspoon chopped fresh
mint leaves**

1 cup marshmallow creme

**1 package (8 oz) ⅓-less-fat
cream cheese (Neufchâtel),
softened**

**Assorted fruit for dipping
(2 cups honeydew balls,
2 kiwifruit, peeled and
sliced, 2 ripe mangoes, cut
into chunks or slices, 2 cups
cantaloupe cubes or slices,
1 pint strawberries)**

Fresh mint leaves, if desired

1 In food processor, place chopped mango and mint. Cover; process about 10 seconds or until smooth.

2 Add marshmallow creme and cream cheese; process about 10 seconds longer or until well blended. Serve with fruit. Garnish with mint leaves.

1 Serving: Calories 110 (Calories from Fat 30); Total Fat 3.5g (Saturated Fat 2g; Trans Fat 0g); Cholesterol 10mg; Sodium 70mg; Total Carbohydrate 18g (Dietary Fiber 1g) **% Daily Value:** Vitamin A 25%; Vitamin C 70%; Calcium 2%; Iron 0% **Exchanges:** ½ Fruit, ½ Other Carbohydrate, ½ High-Fat Meat **Carbohydrate Choices:** 1

Peeled mango strips are often available in the refrigerated section of the produce department. They can be used in place of fresh mango, but their flavor will differ slightly from that of fresh.

Red Pepper Hummus with Pita Chips

 **Superfast**

Prep Time: 10 Minutes

Start to Finish: 10 Minutes

12 servings (2 tablespoons hummus each)

1 can (19 oz) chick peas or garbanzo beans, drained, rinsed

1 tablespoon lemon juice

1 tablespoon olive or canola oil

2 cloves garlic, chopped

⅓ cup drained roasted red bell peppers (from a jar)

Chopped fresh parsley

1 package (7 oz) pita chips

1 In food processor, place chick peas, lemon juice, oil and garlic. Cover; process 1 to 2 minutes or until smooth. Add roasted peppers; process 30 to 60 seconds or until peppers are finely chopped.

2 Place in serving bowl; cover and refrigerate until ready to serve.

3 Sprinkle with parsley. Serve with pita chips.

1 Serving: Calories 140 (Calories from Fat 40); Total Fat 4.5g (Saturated Fat 0g; Trans Fat 0g); Cholesterol 0mg; Sodium 85mg; Total Carbohydrate 21g (Dietary Fiber 4g) **% Daily Value:** Vitamin A 6%; Vitamin C 15%; Calcium 0%; Iron 8% **Exchanges:** 1½ Starch, ½ Fat **Carbohydrate Choices:** 1½

- You can serve this Middle Eastern spread like they do in Turkey—make a depression in the middle of the bowl of hummus, and spoon in a tablespoon of olive oil.

- If a food processor is not available, mash the chick peas with a fork. The mixture may be slightly lumpy, but does not interfere with the wonderful flavor.

tips for dips

Double Duty Dips

Leftover dips can make a great spread for all kinds of hot or cold sandwiches; try sweet and savory spreads. Spread dips on bread and pair them with lean roast beef, a hamburger or leftover chicken.

Tip-Top Dip Tops

To dress up a dish of dip, especially one that has a dull or neutral color, garnish with one or more of the following:

- Minced chopped herbs
- Finely shredded carrots
- Minced red, yellow and/or green bell pepper
- Chopped green onions
- Minced tomato and red onion
- Fat-free sour cream sprinkled with chili powder or paprika or decorated with a small herb sprig

Low-Fat Dippers

Breads

- French bread slices
- Cocktail bread
- Pita chips
- Quartered slices of whole-grain bread

Crackers/chips

- Melba rounds
- Crisp bread
- Reduced-fat and fat-free crackers
- Mini rice cakes
- Baked tortilla or potato chips
- Whole-grain crackers

Vegetables

- Carrots, celery, zucchini, jicama or green, red or yellow bell pepper sticks
- Thick slices of cucumber
- Whole mushrooms, radishes, cherry tomatoes, snow pea pods, sugar snap peas
- Broccoli, cauliflower florets

Chipotle Pico de Gallo

 **Superfast**

Prep Time: 20 Minutes
Start to Finish: 20 Minutes
12 servings (3 cups)

1 cup coarsely chopped unpeeled seedless cucumber

½ cup chopped peeled jicama

½ cup chopped red bell pepper

1 tablespoon lime juice

1 tablespoon honey

¼ teaspoon salt

2 seedless oranges, peeled, coarsely chopped

2 chipotle chiles in adobo sauce (from a can), chopped

12 oz whole-grain tortilla chips

1 In medium bowl, mix all ingredients except chips.

2 Serve immediately with chips, or cover and refrigerate until serving time.

1 Serving (¼ Cup): Calories 160 (Calories from Fat 60); Total Fat 6g (Saturated Fat 0.5g; Trans Fat 0g); Cholesterol 0mg; Sodium 180mg; Total Carbohydrate 25g (Dietary Fiber 3g) **% Daily Value:** Vitamin A 6%; Vitamin C 35%; Calcium 0%; Iron 2% **Exchanges:** 1 Starch, ½ Other Carbohydrate, 1 Fat **Carbohydrate Choices:** 1½

This smoky pico de gallo is excellent with grilled chicken, fish or pork. To turn up the heat, add more adobo. To make this relish less spicy, use just one chipotle chile.

Spanish Salsa with Crispy French Bread

Prep Time: 20 Minutes

Start to Finish:
30 Minutes

16 servings (2 slices bread and ¼ cup salsa each)

BREAD

32 very thin diagonal slices French bread

Cooking spray

SALSA

1 cup finely chopped fresh mushrooms

1 tablespoon chopped fresh parsley

1 tablespoon balsamic or red wine vinegar

2 teaspoons dried basil leaves

¼ teaspoon salt

6 plum (Roma) tomatoes, finely chopped

2 medium green onions, sliced (2 tablespoons)

1 jar (6 oz) marinated artichoke hearts, drained, finely chopped

1 can (4¼ oz) chopped ripe olives, drained

1 Heat oven to 325°F. Line cookie sheet with foil. Place bread slices on cookie sheet; spray lightly with cooking spray. Bake 7 to 10 minutes or until very crisp. Place bread slices on cooling rack; cool completely.

2 Meanwhile, in decorative bowl, mix salsa ingredients. Let stand at room temperature 10 minutes to blend flavors, or cover and refrigerate until serving time. Serve salsa with crispy bread slices.

1 Serving: Calories 30 (Calories from Fat 5); Total Fat 1g (Saturated Fat 0g; Trans Fat 0g); Cholesterol 0mg; Sodium 100mg; Total Carbohydrate 4g (Dietary Fiber 0g) **% Daily Value:** Vitamin A 2%; Vitamin C 4%; Calcium 0%; Iron 2% **Exchanges:** ½ Other Carbohydrate **Carbohydrate Choices:** 0

- Any variety of tomato will work in this recipe. We call for plum (Roma) tomatoes because they are firm in texture and don't contain a lot of seeds.

- Instead of French bread slices, serve this refreshing salsa with tortilla chips.

Hawaiian Appetizer Quesadillas

Prep Time: 20 Minutes

Start to Finish:
30 Minutes

32 appetizers

1 package (11.5 oz) flour
tortillas for burritos
(8 tortillas)

Cooking spray

1 cup finely chopped cooked
Canadian bacon (about 5 oz)

½ cup crushed pineapple
(from 8-oz can), well drained

1 cup finely shredded Mexican
cheese blend (4 oz)

½ cup mango or peach salsa*

1 Move oven rack to lowest position; heat oven to 400°F. Spray
1 side of 4 tortillas with cooking spray. On large cookie sheet,
place tortillas, sprayed sides down, overlapping in center
so tortillas do not hang over edge of sheet. Top evenly with
bacon, pineapple, cheese and remaining tortillas. Spray tops
of tortillas with cooking spray. Place another cookie sheet on
top of tortillas; press down.

2 Place on lowest oven rack; bake 8 to 10 minutes or until
bottom tortillas are golden brown. Turn cookie sheets and
quesadillas over. Bake about 5 minutes longer or until
bottoms are golden brown and cheese is melted. Cut each
into 8 small wedges; serve warm with salsa.

*You can stir fresh mango or peach pieces into salsa if you can't find mango or peach salsa.

1 Appetizer: Calories 60 (Calories from Fat 25); Total Fat 2.5g (Saturated Fat 1g; Trans Fat
0g); Cholesterol 5mg; Sodium 160mg; Total Carbohydrate 7g (Dietary Fiber 0g) **% Daily
Value:** Vitamin A 0%; Vitamin C 0%; Calcium 4%; Iron 2% **Exchanges:** ½ Starch, ½ Fat
Carbohydrate Choices: ½

about quesadillas

Quesadillas (kay-sah-DEE-yahs) take their name from the
Spanish word for cheese, *queso*. At its simplest, this Mexican-
inspired snack is nothing more than cheese melted between
two tortillas and cut into wedges but it's easy to add more
ingredients to vary the flavors. For a bite-size version, roll up
a tortilla with some shredded cheese and a slice of ham and
microwave for about 30 seconds. Slice the roll into one-inch
pieces and serve.

Fresh Tomato-Basil Caprese Kabobs

Prep Time: 30 Minutes

Start to Finish: 30 Minutes

34 kabobs

¼ cup extra-virgin olive oil

2 tablespoons lemon juice

⅔ cup coarsely chopped fresh basil leaves or lemon basil leaves

¼ teaspoon salt

¼ teaspoon freshly ground black pepper

1 pint (2 cups) red cherry tomatoes

1 pint (2 cups) yellow cherry tomatoes

2 medium zucchini or yellow summer squash, cubed

1 lb fresh mozzarella cheese, cubed

34 (6-inch) bamboo skewers

Fresh basil leaves, if desired

1 In large bowl, mix oil, lemon juice, basil, salt and pepper, using wire whisk. Add tomatoes, zucchini and cheese. Cover and refrigerate 10 minutes.

2 Drain vegetables, reserving olive oil mixture. Thread skewers alternately with tomatoes, zucchini and cheese; top with basil leaf. Serve kabobs with reserved olive oil mixture.

1 Kabob: Calories 60 (Calories from Fat 40); Total Fat 4.5g (Saturated Fat 2g; Trans Fat 0g); Cholesterol 5mg; Sodium 90mg; Total Carbohydrate 2g (Dietary Fiber 0g) **% Daily Value:** Vitamin A 8%; Vitamin C 8%; Calcium 10%; Iron 0% **Exchanges:** ½ Vegetable, 1 Fat **Carbohydrate Choices:** 0

Virtually any skewer-able vegetable will work in this recipe. Try red, green or yellow bell pepper pieces or fresh pea pods.

Make ahead for even more flavor.

Meatballs with Fire Roasted Tomato Sauce

Prep Time: 20 Minutes

Start to Finish:
30 Minutes

15 servings
(2 meatballs each)

MEATBALLS

1 lb extra-lean (at least 90%) ground beef

¼ cup unseasoned dry bread crumbs

½ teaspoon garlic salt

¼ teaspoon pepper

4 medium green onions, finely chopped (¼ cup)

1 egg

SAUCE

1 jar (25.5 oz) fire roasted tomato pasta sauce

¾ cup dried cherries, chopped

½ cup water

2 tablespoons cider vinegar or wine vinegar

Chopped fresh chives, if desired

1 Heat oven to 400°F. In large bowl, mix meatball ingredients. Shape into 30 (1-inch) meatballs. Place in ungreased 13×9-inch pan.

2 Bake uncovered about 15 minutes or until thoroughly cooked and no longer pink in center.

3 Meanwhile, in 3-quart saucepan, heat all sauce ingredients except chives to boiling, stirring occasionally; reduce heat. Stir in meatballs. Sprinkle with chives. Serve in chafing dish or slow cooker on Low heat setting.

1 Serving: Calories 110 (Calories from Fat 35); Total Fat 3.5g (Saturated Fat 1g; Trans Fat 0g); Cholesterol 35mg; Sodium 200mg; Total Carbohydrate 11g (Dietary Fiber 1g) **% Daily Value:** Vitamin A 15%; Vitamin C 8%; Calcium 2%; Iron 8% **Exchanges:** 1 Other Carbohydrate, 1 Lean Meat **Carbohydrate Choices:** 1

One can (14.5 oz) fire roasted diced tomatoes can be used instead of the water in the sauce.

Instead of toothpicks, try spearing these meatballs with pretzel sticks.

Margarita Shot-Glass Shrimp

Prep Time: 30 Minutes
Start to Finish: 30 Minutes
24 appetizers

Lime wedges, if desired

Coarse salt, if desired

Coarse ground black pepper, if desired

1 cup zesty cocktail sauce

½ cup finely chopped red or yellow bell pepper

1 tablespoon lime juice

2 cans (8 oz each) crushed pineapple in juice, drained

24 cooked deveined peeled large shrimp (about 2 lb)

Cilantro sprigs, if desired

1 Rub rims of 24 (2-oz) cordial glasses (shot glasses) with lime wedges; dip rims in coarse salt and pepper.

2 In medium bowl, mix cocktail sauce, bell pepper, lime juice and pineapple. Place about 1 tablespoon sauce mixture in bottom of each glass. Place 1 shrimp in each glass; top each with lime wedge and cilantro sprig. Serve immediately, or cover and refrigerate until serving time.

Alternative Method: In medium bowl, mix cocktail sauce, bell pepper, lime juice and pineapple. Serve immediately, or cover and refrigerate until serving time. To serve, spoon cocktail sauce mixture into small serving bowl; place on serving tray. Arrange shrimp around bowl of sauce. Garnish with lime wedges and cilantro sprigs.

1 Appetizer: Calories 40 (Calories from Fat 0); Total Fat 0g (Saturated Fat 0g; Trans Fat 0g); Cholesterol 35mg; Sodium 170mg; Total Carbohydrate 5g (Dietary Fiber 0g) **% Daily Value:** Vitamin A 6%; Vitamin C 15%; Calcium 0%; Iron 4% **Exchanges:** ½ Other Carbohydrate, ½ Very Lean Meat **Carbohydrate Choices:** ½

Buy plastic disposable shot glasses at a party supply store if you don't have enough glass ones.

Regular seafood cocktail sauce plus ⅛ teaspoon ground red pepper (cayenne) can be used in place of the zesty cocktail sauce.

Crispy Shrimp Tarts

See photo, page 10

Prep Time: 25 Minutes

Start to Finish:
30 Minutes

24 appetizers

24 frozen mini fillo shells
(from two 2.1-oz packages)

½ cup cream cheese spread
(from 8-oz container)

24 frozen cooked deveined
peeled medium shrimp

¼ cup Chinese plum sauce

Grated lime peel, if desired

1 Heat oven to 350°F. Place fillo shells on ungreased large cookie sheet.

2 Stir cream cheese to soften. Spoon 1 teaspoon cream cheese into each shell. Top each with 1 shrimp.

3 Bake about 2 minutes or until cream cheese is soft. Remove from cookie sheet; place on serving platter. Top each with ½ teaspoon plum sauce and lime peel.

1 Appetizer: Calories 40 (Calories from Fat 20); Total Fat 2.5g (Saturated Fat 1g; Trans Fat 0g); Cholesterol 15mg; Sodium 60mg; Total Carbohydrate 3g (Dietary Fiber 0g) **% Daily Value:** Vitamin A 0%; Vitamin C 0%; Calcium 0%; Iron 0% **Exchanges:** ½ Medium-Fat Meat **Carbohydrate Choices:** 0

- Plum sauce, also called duck sauce, is made from plums, apricots and seasonings. Thick and sweet, plum sauce is a traditional condiment for duck, pork or spareribs.

- Cooked crabmeat can be used in place of the shrimp.

Cucumber-Hummus Stacks

 **Superfast**

Prep Time: 20 Minutes

Start to Finish:
20 Minutes

26 appetizers

1 large cucumber (about 12 oz), unpeeled

1 container (7 oz) roasted red pepper hummus

2 tablespoons crumbled feta cheese

26 slices kalamata or ripe olives

1 Using tines of fork, score cucumber lengthwise on all sides. Cut cucumber into 26 (¼-inch) slices. Blot dry with paper towel.

2 Spoon heaping teaspoon hummus on each cucumber slice. Sprinkle with feta cheese; top with olive slice.

1 Appetizer: Calories 20 (Calories from Fat 10); Total Fat 1g (Saturated Fat 0g; Trans Fat 0g); Cholesterol 0mg; Sodium 55mg; Total Carbohydrate 2g (Dietary Fiber 0g) **% Daily Value:** Vitamin A 0%; Vitamin C 0%; Calcium 0%; Iron 2% **Exchanges:** Free **Carbohydrate Choices:** 0

- Hummus comes in a variety of flavors; try these stacks with your favorite.

- If choosing a burpless cucumber, buy one that weighs at least 20 ounces.

Garlic Cream and Tomato Crostini

 **Superfast**

Prep Time: 15 Minutes

Start to Finish:
15 Minutes

20 crostini

20 slices French bread
(½ inch)

1 tablespoon olive or
vegetable oil

½ cup garlic-and-herb cream
cheese spread (from 8-oz
container)

4 medium green onions,
chopped (¼ cup)

1 tablespoon chopped fresh
thyme leaves

2 medium fresh plum (Roma)
tomatoes, chopped

1 Set oven control to broil. On ungreased cookie sheet, place bread slices. Lightly brush each with oil. Broil with tops 4 to 6 inches from heat about 1 minute or until light golden brown.

2 In small bowl, mix cream cheese and green onions. Spread mixture on toasted bread slices. Broil about 1 minute longer or until cream cheese bubbles. Sprinkle thyme leaves and tomatoes over top.

1 Crostini: Calories 50 (Calories from Fat 25); Total Fat 3g (Saturated Fat 1.5g; Trans Fat 0g); Cholesterol 5mg; Sodium 70mg; Total Carbohydrate 5g (Dietary Fiber 0g) **% Daily Value:** Vitamin A 0%; Vitamin C 0%; Calcium 0%; Iron 2% **Exchanges:** ½ Starch, ½ Fat **Carbohydrate Choices:** ½

- Garlic-and-herb cream cheese spread is soft cream cheese found near the regular cream cheese in the grocery store.

- To make ahead, toast bread, and cool completely before storing in an airtight food-storage plastic bag. Just before serving, spread crostini with cream cheese mixture, and broil.

Fresh Sugar Snap Peas with Sesame

 **Superfast**

Prep Time: 10 Minutes

Start to Finish:
10 Minutes

**12 servings (4 snap
pea pods each)**

1 teaspoon soy sauce

¼ **teaspoon roasted
sesame oil**

1 bag (8 oz) fresh sugar snap
peas, ends trimmed (2 cups)

½ **teaspoon black sesame
seed**

1 In medium bowl, mix soy sauce and oil. Add peas; stir to coat.

2 Arrange on serving platter; sprinkle with sesame seed. Serve with toothpicks.

1 Serving: Calories 10 (Calories from Fat 0); Total Fat 0g (Saturated Fat 0g; Trans Fat 0g); Cholesterol 0mg; Sodium 30mg; Total Carbohydrate 0g (Dietary Fiber 0g) **% Daily Value:** Vitamin A 4%; Vitamin C 20%; Calcium 0%; Iron 0% **Exchanges:** Free **Carbohydrate Choices:** 0

- Black sesame seed is used in Japanese dishes. Its aroma and flavor is stronger than that of white sesame seed.

- You can use white sesame seed instead of black sesame seed. For better flavor, toast just before use in heavy ungreased pan over medium heat. Toast about one minute while shaking pan occasionally. Remove from heat and serve.

Microwave Dill Tater Snacks  Superfast

Prep Time: 20 Minutes
Start to Finish:
20 Minutes
20 appetizers

3 slices lean turkey bacon

10 small red potatoes, unpeeled, halved (about 1½ lb)

½ cup reduced-fat sour cream

2 medium green onions, sliced (2 tablespoons)

1 teaspoon chopped fresh dill weed

Dash pepper

¼ cup grated Parmesan cheese

Fresh dill weed or parsley, if desired

1 Cook bacon in microwave as directed on package. Cool slightly. Crumble; set aside.

2 Place potatoes, cut side down, in 12×8-inch (2-quart) ungreased microwavable dish. Add 2 tablespoons water. Cover tightly with microwavable plastic wrap.

3 Microwave on High 9 to 12 minutes or until tender, rotating dish ¼ turn halfway through cooking. Let stand 3 minutes. Drain; cool slightly.

4 In small bowl, mix sour cream, onions and 1 teaspoon dill weed. Turn potatoes over. If necessary, trim thin slice off rounded bottom of each potato half to make potatoes stand upright. Top each with dollop of sour cream mixture; sprinkle with bacon. Sprinkle each with pepper and Parmesan cheese. Garnish with fresh dill weed or parsley.

1 Appetizer: Calories 45 (Calories from Fat 10); Total Fat 1g (Saturated Fat 0.5g; Trans Fat 0g); Cholesterol 0mg; Sodium 45mg; Total Carbohydrate 6g (Dietary Fiber 0g) **% Daily Value:** Vitamin A 0%; Vitamin C 4%; Calcium 2%; Iron 4% **Exchanges:** ½ Starch **Carbohydrate Choices:** ½

Besides being a tasty appetizer, these potatoes are also a great side dish for roasted meat or poultry. If a 12×8-inch dish will not fit in your microwave oven, use a microwavable pie plate, and cook half the potatoes at a time. Microwave on High six to eight minutes or until tender.

skillet meals and casseroles

chapter

2

Beef Fried Rice, see page 40

Beef Fried Rice

See photo, page 38

Prep Time: 30 Minutes

Start to Finish:
30 Minutes

6 servings (1⅓ cups each)

1 cup uncooked regular long-grain white rice

2 cups water

1 teaspoon olive oil

1 egg, beaten

1 lb extra-lean (at least 90%) ground beef

1 cup sliced fresh mushrooms

½ cup sliced celery

⅓ cup reduced-sodium soy sauce

2 teaspoons sesame oil

½ teaspoon red pepper sauce

1½ cups fresh snow pea pods, cut diagonally in half

8 medium green onions, chopped (½ cup)

1 Cook rice in water as directed on package.

2 Meanwhile, brush 12-inch nonstick skillet with olive oil. Heat over medium heat. Add beaten egg to skillet; cook 1 minute or until firm but still moist. Remove from skillet; cut into thin strips. Cover to keep warm.

3 In same skillet, cook beef, mushrooms and celery over medium heat 8 to 10 minutes, stirring frequently, until beef is thoroughly cooked.

4 In small bowl, mix soy sauce, sesame oil and pepper sauce; stir into beef mixture. Add pea pods, onions, cooked egg and cooked rice; cook 2 to 3 minutes longer, stirring constantly, until hot.

1 Serving: Calories 290 (Calories from Fat 90); Total Fat 10g (Saturated Fat 3g; Trans Fat 0g); Cholesterol 80mg; Sodium 530mg; Total Carbohydrate 30g (Dietary Fiber 1g) **% Daily Value:** Vitamin A 6%; Vitamin C 10%; Calcium 4%; Iron 20% **Exchanges:** 2 Starch, 2 Lean Meat, ½ Fat **Carbohydrate Choices:** 2

Light-colored sesame oil adds a delicate nutty flavor to salad dressings, sautés or stir-fries. Dark sesame oil has a rich aroma that makes it perfect for flavoring finished recipes. Use either light or dark sesame oil in this fried rice.

Pepper-Rubbed Steaks with Caramelized Onions

 **Superfast**

Prep Time: 20 Minutes
Start to Finish:
20 Minutes
4 servings

1 large sweet onion (Maui, Texas Sweet or Walla Walla), thinly sliced, separated into rings

1 tablespoon sugar

2 tablespoons water

1 tablespoon balsamic vinegar

½ to 1 teaspoon seasoned pepper blend

4 boneless beef strip steaks, ½ to ¾ inch thick (4 oz each), trimmed of fat

1 Heat 12-inch nonstick skillet over medium heat. Add onion; cook 3 to 4 minutes, stirring frequently, just until it begins to brown. Stir in sugar and water. Reduce heat to medium-low; cover and cook 6 to 8 minutes, stirring frequently, until onion is tender and golden. Remove from heat; stir in vinegar.

2 Meanwhile, heat closed contact grill for 5 minutes. Rub pepper blend on both sides of each steak.

3 When grill is heated, place steaks on bottom grill surface. Close grill; cook 3 to 5 minutes or until desired doneness. Serve steaks with onions.

1 Serving: Calories 190 (Calories from Fat 35); Total Fat 4g (Saturated Fat 1.5g; Trans Fat 0g); Cholesterol 75mg; Sodium 40mg; Total Carbohydrate 7g (Dietary Fiber 0g) **% Daily Value:** Vitamin A 0%; Vitamin C 2%; Calcium 0%; Iron 15% **Exchanges:** ½ Other Carbohydrate, 4 Very Lean Meat, ½ Fat **Carbohydrate Choices:** ½

You don't have to give up red meat completely to eat a healthful diet; just eat less of it. Lean beef contains iron, folic acid and vitamin B12, all important nutrients.

Beef with Burgundy Mushrooms

Prep Time: 25 Minutes
Start to Finish: 25 Minutes
4 servings

2 cups uncooked medium egg noodles (4 oz)

1 lb boneless beef sirloin steak (½ inch thick), cut into 4 pieces

2 packages (8 oz each) fresh whole mushrooms, quartered

1 can (10½ oz) condensed French onion soup

¼ cup dry red wine (such as Burgundy) or nonalcoholic wine

1 tablespoon cornstarch

3 tablespoons tomato paste with basil, garlic and oregano

½ teaspoon dried oregano leaves

2 tablespoons chopped fresh parsley

Pepper

1 Cook and drain noodles as directed on package, omitting salt. Place in serving bowl; cover to keep warm.

2 Meanwhile, heat 12-inch nonstick skillet over medium-high heat. Add beef; cook 3 to 4 minutes on each side or until desired doneness. Remove from heat. Place beef on serving platter; cover to keep warm.

3 Wipe skillet clean with paper towels. Heat skillet again over medium-high heat. Add mushrooms; cook 10 minutes, stirring occasionally.

4 Meanwhile, in medium bowl, mix soup, wine, cornstarch, tomato paste and oregano.

5 Add soup mixture to mushrooms; cook, stirring frequently, until bubbly and thickened. Remove from heat. Stir in parsley, and season to taste with pepper. Spoon mushroom mixture over beef; serve with noodles.

1 Serving: Calories 350 (Calories from Fat 70); Total Fat 8g (Saturated Fat 2g; Trans Fat 0g); Cholesterol 95mg; Sodium 720mg; Total Carbohydrate 32g (Dietary Fiber 3g) **% Daily Value:** Vitamin A 8%; Vitamin C 8%; Calcium 4%; Iron 30% **Exchanges:** 1½ Starch, ½ Other Carbohydrate, 4½ Very Lean Meat, 1 Fat **Carbohydrate Choices:** 2

Lemony Pork Primavera Pasta

Prep Time: 30 Minutes
Start to Finish:
30 Minutes

4 servings (2 cups each)

6 oz uncooked fettuccine or linguine

1 lb boneless pork loin chops (¾ inch thick)

1 tablespoon olive or canola oil

2 cups fresh broccoli florets (about 5 oz)

4 oz fresh green beans, trimmed, cut into 1-inch pieces (about 1 cup)

1 medium red bell pepper, cut into 1½×¼-inch strips

⅓ cup lemon juice

⅓ cup water

2 tablespoons sugar

1 tablespoon cornstarch

½ teaspoon salt

1 Cook and drain fettuccine as directed on package.

2 Meanwhile, cut pork into 2×¾×¼-inch strips. In 12-inch nonstick skillet, heat oil over medium-high heat. Add pork, broccoli, green beans and bell pepper; cook 6 to 8 minutes, stirring frequently, until pork is no longer pink in center and vegetables are crisp-tender.

3 In small bowl, mix remaining ingredients until smooth. Stir into pork mixture. Cook 1 to 2 minutes, stirring constantly, until bubbly and thickened.

4 Stir cooked fettuccine into sauce mixture; cook, stirring occasionally, until hot.

1 Serving: Calories 430 (Calories from Fat 130); Total Fat 15g (Saturated Fat 4g; Trans Fat 0g); Cholesterol 100mg; Sodium 540mg; Total Carbohydrate 44g (Dietary Fiber 4g) **% Daily Value:** Vitamin A 30%; Vitamin C 70%; Calcium 6%; Iron 20% **Exchanges:** 2 Starch, ½ Other Carbohydrate, 1 Vegetable, 3 Lean Meat, 1 Fat **Carbohydrate Choices:** 3

Prepare all the vegetables and cut the pork up to four hours ahead of time. Cover and refrigerate. When you're ready to eat, dinner is just 10 minutes away!

Barbecued Pork Fajitas

 **Superfast**

Prep Time: 20 Minutes
Start to Finish:
20 Minutes
4 fajitas

1 teaspoon ground cumin

½ teaspoon garlic-pepper blend

1 lb boneless pork loin chops, cut into thin bite-size strips

½ medium red bell pepper, cut into thin bite-size strips

½ medium green bell pepper, cut into thin bite-size strips

½ cup red onion slices or 1 medium onion, sliced

⅓ cup barbecue sauce

4 fat-free flour tortillas (8 to 10 inch)

1 In resealable food-storage plastic bag, place cumin and garlic-pepper blend. Seal bag; shake to blend. Add pork; seal bag and shake to coat.

2 Heat 10-inch nonstick skillet over medium-high heat. Add pork; cook and stir 2 minutes.

3 Add bell peppers and onion; cook 2 to 3 minutes, stirring frequently, until pork is no longer pink in center and vegetables are crisp-tender. Stir in barbecue sauce; cook and stir until hot. Serve pork mixture in tortillas.

1 Fajita: Calories 390 (Calories from Fat 80); Total Fat 9g (Saturated Fat 3g; Trans Fat 0g); Cholesterol 70mg; Sodium 720mg; Total Carbohydrate 45g (Dietary Fiber 4g) **% Daily Value:** Vitamin A 10%; Vitamin C 30%; Calcium 8%; Iron 20% **Exchanges:** 2½ Starch, ½ Other Carbohydrate, 3 Lean Meat **Carbohydrate Choices:** 3

meat: nutrition facts

Beef, pork and lamb are excellent sources of protein and iron as well as zinc, phosphorus, thiamine, riboflavin, niacin and vitamins B6 and B12. When eaten in moderation, meat makes a substantial contribution to a well-balanced diet. Some tips:

- Figure three to four ounces of meat per person.

- Trim visible fat before cooking.

- Choose cooking methods that do not add fat, such as broiling, roasting, grilling, braising and stewing.

- Stretch a small amount of meat in a main dish with lots of vegetables, grains and/or pasta.

Weeknight Pork and Vegetable Stew

Prep Time: 30 Minutes

Start to Finish:
30 Minutes

4 servings (1¼ cups each)

1 teaspoon canola oil

¾ lb pork tenderloin, cut into 1-inch cubes

½ teaspoon salt

⅛ teaspoon pepper

1 cup frozen small whole onions (from 1-lb bag)

1 tablespoon ketchup

1 teaspoon dried rosemary leaves, crushed

½ teaspoon chopped garlic in water (from 4.5-oz jar)

1 bag (1 lb) frozen broccoli, carrots and cauliflower

1 jar (12 oz) pork gravy

1 In 3-quart saucepan, heat oil over medium-high heat. Add pork; sprinkle with salt and pepper. Cook 3 to 5 minutes, stirring frequently, until pork is browned.

2 Stir in remaining ingredients. Heat to boiling. Reduce heat to low; cover and simmer 15 to 20 minutes, stirring occasionally, until vegetables are tender and pork is no longer pink in center.

1 Serving: Calories 230 (Calories from Fat 60); Total Fat 7g (Saturated Fat 2.5g; Trans Fat 0g); Cholesterol 55mg; Sodium 870mg; Total Carbohydrate 16g (Dietary Fiber 4g) **% Daily Value:** Vitamin A 50%; Vitamin C 35%; Calcium 6%; Iron 15% **Exchanges:** ½ Other Carbohydrate, 1 Vegetable, 3 Lean Meat **Carbohydrate Choices:** 1

To get a variety of nutrients, some experts recommend eating a colorful array of fruits and vegetables. This stew provides orange, green and white vegetables.

stretching soup or stew

Soup is the thrifty cook's dream; you can almost always "throw something in" to use up leftovers or stretch the meal for an unexpected guest or two. Check your freezer, refrigerator and pantry for last-minute add-ins:

- Frozen corn, beans, peas or leftover cooked vegetables
- Leftover rice or pasta

- Chopped tomatoes or fresh salsa
- Coleslaw mix
- Shredded spinach, bok choy or other greens

- Chopped leftover chicken, turkey, beef or ham
- Chopped-up carrots, celery, bell pepper slices and green onions
- Leftover noodles
- A cup or so of pasta sauce
- Grated or shredded Parmesan cheese
- Canned drained red kidney, black or canellini beans

Dress up a cup or bowl of soup with one or more of the following:

- Minced fresh herbs
- Chopped green onions
- Oyster crackers or fish-shaped crackers
- Melba toast with melted shredded low-fat mozzarella or another cheese
- Popcorn

- A dollop of nonfat plain yogurt and a basil leaf
- Beaten egg white, stirred into a piping hot clear soup just before it's ladled out for a lower-fat egg-drop soup effect

Southwestern Pork and Black Bean Stir-Fry

Prep Time: 30 Minutes

Start to Finish:
30 Minutes

4 servings (1½ cups each)

1 tablespoon olive or canola oil

¾ lb pork tenderloin, cut into 2×½×¼-inch strips

1 medium onion, cut into thin wedges

1 small red bell pepper, cut into thin bite-size strips

2 cloves garlic, finely chopped

2 cups frozen whole kernel corn, thawed*

1 can (15 oz) black beans, drained, rinsed

1 small zucchini, chopped (about 1 cup)

½ cup chunky-style salsa

1 In 10-inch nonstick skillet, heat oil over medium-high heat. Add pork, onion, bell pepper and garlic; cook 6 to 8 minutes, stirring frequently, until pork is no longer pink in center and vegetables are crisp-tender.

2 Stir in remaining ingredients. Reduce heat to medium; cover and simmer 5 to 7 minutes, stirring occasionally, until zucchini is crisp-tender and flavors are blended. If desired, season to taste with salt and pepper.

*To quickly thaw corn, place in colander or strainer; rinse with warm water until thawed. Drain well.

1 Serving: Calories 380 (Calories from Fat 70); Total Fat 8g (Saturated Fat 2g; Trans Fat 0g); Cholesterol 55mg; Sodium 240mg; Total Carbohydrate 46g (Dietary Fiber 13g) **% Daily Value:** Vitamin A 20%; Vitamin C 30%; Calcium 10%; Iron 20% **Exchanges:** 2 Starch, ½ Other Carbohydrate, 1 Vegetable, 3 Lean Meat **Carbohydrate Choices:** 3

Black beans are an excellent source of protein and are high in fiber. This recipe also includes red bell pepper, which is rich in vitamins A and C.

Orange Chicken Stir-Fry

 **Superfast**

Prep Time: 10 Minutes
Start to Finish:
20 Minutes
4 servings (2¼ cups each)

2 cups uncooked instant rice

2 cups water

3 tablespoons frozen
(thawed) orange juice
concentrate

2 tablespoons low-sodium soy
sauce

½ teaspoon cornstarch

¼ teaspoon garlic powder

1 lb chicken breast strips for
stir-fry

1 bag (1 lb) frozen broccoli,
carrots and water chestnuts,
thawed, drained*

Chopped green onions, if
desired

1 Cook rice in water as directed on package, omitting salt.

2 Meanwhile, in small bowl, mix orange juice concentrate, soy
sauce, cornstarch and garlic powder until smooth.

3 Heat 10-inch nonstick skillet over medium-high heat. Add
chicken; cook 5 to 8 minutes, stirring frequently, until
chicken is no longer pink in center.

4 Stir in juice concentrate mixture and vegetables. Reduce
heat to medium; cover and cook 6 to 8 minutes, stirring
occasionally, until vegetables are crisp-tender. Serve over
rice. Garnish with onions.

*To quickly thaw frozen vegetables, place them in a colander or strainer and rinse with
warm water until thawed. Drain very well.

1 Serving: Calories 390 (Calories from Fat 45); Total Fat 5g (Saturated Fat 1g; Trans Fat
0g); Cholesterol 70mg; Sodium 340mg; Total Carbohydrate 55g (Dietary Fiber 4g) **% Daily
Value:** Vitamin A 25%; Vitamin C 45%; Calcium 6%; Iron 30% **Exchanges:** 2½ Starch,
1 Other Carbohydrate, 1 Vegetable, 3 Very Lean Meat **Carbohydrate Choices:** 3½

Caribbean Chicken and Pineapple Salsa

Prep Time: 15 Minutes

Start to Finish: 30 Minutes

4 servings

CHICKEN

1¼ cups Fiber One® cereal

2 teaspoons jerk seasoning (dry)

4 boneless skinless chicken breasts (about 1¼ lb)

½ cup buttermilk

2 teaspoons Dijon mustard

½ teaspoon red pepper sauce

PINEAPPLE SALSA

1 can (8 oz) crushed pineapple in juice, undrained

¼ cup chopped red bell pepper

¼ cup chopped apricots or papaya, if desired

1 tablespoon chopped fresh cilantro

1 teaspoon sugar

1 teaspoon lemon juice

1 Heat oven to 400°F. Spray cookie sheet with cooking spray. Place cereal in resealable food-storage plastic bag; seal bag and finely crush with rolling pin or meat mallet (or crush in food processor). Place cereal in shallow dish. Stir in jerk seasoning.

2 In large resealable food-storage plastic bag, place chicken, buttermilk, mustard and pepper sauce. Seal bag; shake well. Remove chicken from bag; coat with cereal mixture. Place on cookie sheet.

3 Bake 14 to 16 minutes or until juice of chicken is clear when center of thickest part is cut (170°F). Meanwhile, mix salsa ingredients. Cover; refrigerate until serving time. Serve with chicken.

1 Serving: Calories 300 (Calories from Fat 50); Total Fat 6g (Saturated Fat 1.5g; Trans Fat 0g); Cholesterol 85mg; Sodium 380mg; Total Carbohydrate 28g (Dietary Fiber 9g) **% Daily Value:** Vitamin A 15%; Vitamin C 20%; Calcium 10%; Iron 25% **Exchanges:** 1 Starch, 1 Other Carbohydrate, 4 Very Lean Meat, ½ Fat **Carbohydrate Choices:** 2

Thirty-minute dinner! Dijon and jerk seasoning jazz up baked chicken breasts while bran cereal adds crunch. A peppy fruit salsa makes a sassy topper.

Fruits offer a host of nutrients including vitamin C to accompany their great taste. Be sure to get at least two to three servings of fruit daily.

Lemon-Basil Skillet Chicken with Rice

 **Superfast**

Prep Time: 10 Minutes

Start to Finish:
20 Minutes

4 servings

1 teaspoon canola oil

4 boneless skinless chicken breasts (1 lb)

Paprika

1½ cups hot water

1½ cups uncooked instant brown rice

2 tablespoons butter or margarine

1 tablespoon lemon juice

1 teaspoon dried basil leaves

¼ teaspoon salt

1 In 10-inch nonstick skillet, heat oil over high heat. Sprinkle both sides of chicken breasts with paprika; add to hot skillet. Immediately reduce heat to medium-high; cover and cook 4 minutes.

2 Meanwhile, in 2-quart saucepan, place hot water; cover tightly. Heat to boiling. Stir in rice; remove from heat. Let stand 5 minutes.

3 Turn chicken; cover and cook 4 to 5 minutes longer or until juice of chicken is clear when center of thickest part is cut (170°F). Remove chicken from skillet; place on serving platter. Cover to keep warm.

4 In same hot skillet, mix butter, lemon juice, basil and salt. If necessary, return to heat to melt butter.

5 Place rice on serving platter; arrange chicken over rice. Spoon butter mixture over chicken.

1 Serving: Calories 330 (Calories from Fat 90); Total Fat 11g (Saturated Fat 4.5g; Trans Fat 0g); Cholesterol 85mg; Sodium 540mg; Total Carbohydrate 32g (Dietary Fiber 1g) **% Daily Value:** Vitamin A 6%; Vitamin C 0%; Calcium 0%; Iron 6% **Exchanges:** 2 Starch, 3 Lean Meat **Carbohydrate Choices:** 2

To shave off a few minutes of cook time, use a mallet or rolling pin to pound the chicken breasts to an even thickness.

Honey-Mustard Chicken and Carrots

Prep Time: 25 Minutes
Start to Finish: 25 Minutes
4 servings

2 teaspoons canola or olive oil

4 boneless skinless chicken breasts (1 lb)

½ cup apple juice

2 cups ready-to-eat baby-cut carrots

2 tablespoons sweet honey mustard

3 tablespoons coarsely chopped honey-roasted peanuts

1 In 10-inch nonstick skillet, heat oil over medium-high heat. Add chicken; cook 5 to 8 minutes, turning once, until chicken is browned on both sides.

2 Add apple juice. Reduce heat to medium; cover and cook 5 minutes. Add carrots; cover and cook 5 to 10 minutes longer or until chicken is fork-tender, its juices run clear when center of thickest part is cut (170°F) and carrots are crisp-tender.

3 With slotted spoon, remove chicken and carrots from skillet; place on serving platter and cover to keep warm. Stir mustard into liquid in skillet. Spoon mustard sauce over chicken and carrots; sprinkle with peanuts.

1 Serving: Calories 250 (Calories from Fat 90); Total Fat 10g (Saturated Fat 2g; Trans Fat 0g); Cholesterol 75mg; Sodium 150mg; Total Carbohydrate 12g (Dietary Fiber 2g) **% Daily Value:** Vitamin A 210%; Vitamin C 4%; Calcium 4%; Iron 8% **Exchanges:** ½ Other Carbohydrate, 1 Vegetable, 3½ Lean Meat **Carbohydrate Choices:** 1

The majority of the fat in peanuts is monounsaturated fat, which may help maintain heart health. Just watch portion sizes since peanuts are high in calories.

Chicken with Dijon-Tarragon Cream Sauce

Prep Time: 25 Minutes

Start to Finish: 25 Minutes

4 servings (1½ cups each)

8 oz uncooked fettuccine

1 tablespoon canola or olive oil

1 lb boneless skinless chicken breasts, cut into ½-inch pieces

¾ cup reduced-fat sour cream

½ cup fat-free (skim) milk

2 tablespoons Dijon mustard

1 tablespoon chopped fresh tarragon or 1 teaspoon dried tarragon leaves

2 tablespoons chopped fresh parsley, if desired

1 Cook and drain fettuccine as directed on package.

2 Meanwhile, in 10-inch skillet, heat oil over medium heat. Add chicken; cook 8 to 10 minutes, stirring frequently, until no longer pink in center.

3 In small bowl, mix sour cream, milk and mustard until smooth. Stir in tarragon. Pour into skillet with chicken. Cook about 5 minutes, stirring frequently, until hot. Serve chicken mixture over fettuccine; sprinkle with parsley.

1 Serving: Calories 450 (Calories from Fat 140); Total Fat 16g (Saturated Fat 5g; Trans Fat 0g); Cholesterol 130mg; Sodium 530mg; Total Carbohydrate 42g (Dietary Fiber 2g) **% Daily Value:** Vitamin A 8%; Vitamin C 0%; Calcium 15%; Iron 20% **Exchanges:** 2 Starch, 1 Other Carbohydrate, 4 Lean Meat, ½ Fat **Carbohydrate Choices:** 3

Serve with a salad of baby spinach, sliced fresh strawberries or mandarin orange segments topped with poppy seed dressing.

Turkey Scaloppine with Lemon Sauce

 **Superfast**

Prep Time: 15 Minutes

Start to Finish:
15 Minutes

6 servings

COUSCOUS

1 cup uncooked whole wheat couscous

1½ cups water

SAUCE

2 teaspoons all-purpose flour

¼ teaspoon salt

⅛ teaspoon dried thyme leaves

1 cup fat-free (skim) milk

1 teaspoon all-natural butter-flavor granules

¼ teaspoon grated lemon peel

TURKEY

6 uncooked turkey breast slices (about 1 lb)

¼ teaspoon salt

⅛ teaspoon pepper

1 tablespoon butter or margarine

2 tablespoons chopped fresh parsley

1 Cook couscous in water as directed on package, omitting oil; cover to keep warm.

2 Meanwhile, in 1-quart saucepan, mix flour, ¼ teaspoon salt, the thyme and milk until smooth. Cook over medium-high heat, stirring constantly, until bubbly and thickened. Remove from heat. Stir in butter-flavor granules and lemon peel until well blended; cover to keep warm.

3 Sprinkle both sides of turkey breast slices with ¼ teaspoon salt and the pepper. In 10-inch nonstick skillet, melt butter over medium-high heat. Add turkey; cook 2 to 3 minutes, turning once, until no longer pink in center. Serve turkey slices with sauce over couscous; sprinkle with parsley.

1 Serving: Calories 230 (Calories from Fat 30); Total Fat 3g (Saturated Fat 1.5g; Trans Fat 0g); Cholesterol 55mg; Sodium 260mg; Total Carbohydrate 27g (Dietary Fiber 2g) **% Daily Value:** Vitamin A 4%; Vitamin C 0%; Calcium 8%; Iron 10% **Exchanges:** 2 Starch, 2 Very Lean Meat **Carbohydrate Choices:** 2

Couscous is the perfect pasta for fast dinners because it is so small and cooks in no time. Another benefit—kids just love it!

Asparagus, Shrimp and Dill Fettuccine

Prep Time: 25 Minutes

Start to Finish:
25 Minutes

2 servings

6 oz uncooked fettuccine

¾ cup chicken broth

1 tablespoon all-purpose or unbleached flour

1 tablespoon fresh lemon juice

1½ teaspoons finely chopped fresh dill weed

2 teaspoons olive oil

1 cup cut (1-inch) fresh asparagus spears

½ lb uncooked deveined peeled medium shrimp

2 lemon wedges

1 Cook and drain fettuccine as directed on package. Cover to keep warm.

2 Meanwhile, in small bowl, mix broth and flour. Stir in lemon juice and dill. Set aside.

3 In 10-inch nonstick skillet or Dutch oven, heat olive oil over medium heat until hot. Add asparagus; cook and stir 2 minutes. Add shrimp; cook and stir 3 minutes longer or until shrimp turn pink.

4 Add broth mixture to skillet; cook over medium heat, stirring frequently, until slightly thickened.

5 Add cooked fettuccine to skillet; toss gently to coat. Garnish each serving with lemon wedge.

1 Serving: Calories 470 (Calories from Fat 100); Total Fat 11g (Saturated Fat 2g; Trans Fat 0g); Cholesterol 225mg; Sodium 940mg; Total Carbohydrate 63g (Dietary Fiber 4g) **% Daily Value:** Vitamin A 15%; Vitamin C 10%; Calcium 8%; Iron 45% **Exchanges:** 4 Starch, 1 Vegetable, 2½ Lean Meat **Carbohydrate Choices:** 4

Fresh, uncooked shrimp can be tightly covered and refrigerated for up to two days. Rinse with cold water and pat dry on paper towels before storing.

Crispy Oven-Baked Fish

Prep Time: 10 Minutes
Start to Finish:
30 Minutes
2 servings

1 egg or 1 egg white

1 teaspoon water

⅓ cup Italian-style dry bread crumbs

½ teaspoon lemon-pepper seasoning

¼ teaspoon garlic salt

2 catfish or tilapia fillets (3 to 4 oz each)

Cooking spray

4 lemon wedges

1 Heat oven to 400°F. Line cookie sheet with foil; generously spray foil with cooking spray. In shallow bowl or dish, beat egg and water with wire whisk until well blended. In another shallow bowl or dish, mix bread crumbs, lemon-pepper seasoning and garlic salt.

2 Dip fish into egg mixture; coat with bread crumb mixture. Place on cookie sheet. Spray fish with cooking spray.

3 Bake 10 minutes. Turn fillets; bake 5 to 10 minutes longer or until fish flakes easily with fork. Place fillets on serving platter; garnish with lemon wedges.

1 Serving: Calories 240 (Calories from Fat 90); Total Fat 10g (Saturated Fat 2.5g; Trans Fat 0g); Cholesterol 170mg; Sodium 700mg; Total Carbohydrate 15g (Dietary Fiber 1g) **% Daily Value:** Vitamin A 4%; Vitamin C 8%; Calcium 8%; Iron 15% **Exchanges:** 1 Starch, 3 Lean Meat **Carbohydrate Choices:** 1

dressing up plain fish

Pan-fry or broil flounder, sole or other thin fillets for a supper that's ready in minutes. To dress up plain fish, try:

- A squeeze of fresh lemon or lime
- A dollop of purchased or homemade salsa
- A splash of bottled Italian dressing
- A sprinkle of minced fresh herbs, such as lemon basil and chives
- A topping of quick "cocktail sauce" made by blending ketchup, lemon juice and horseradish
- A bit of chutney

Skillet Fish with Quick Corn Relish

 **Superfast**

Prep Time: 15 Minutes

Start to Finish:
15 Minutes

4 servings

RELISH

1 can (11 oz) whole kernel corn with red and green peppers, drained, rinsed

2 medium green onions, sliced (2 tablespoons)

2 tablespoons chopped fresh cilantro

1 tablespoon lime juice

1 teaspoon honey

½ teaspoon ground cumin

FISH

¼ teaspoon ground cumin

⅛ teaspoon pepper

4 cod or halibut fillets (1 lb)

1 In medium bowl, mix relish ingredients; set aside.

2 In small bowl, mix ¼ teaspoon cumin and the pepper; sprinkle on both sides of each fish fillet.

3 Heat 12-inch nonstick skillet over medium-high heat. Add fish; cook 5 to 8 minutes, turning once, until fish flakes easily with fork. Serve fish with relish.

1 Serving: Calories 180 (Calories from Fat 20); Total Fat 2g (Saturated Fat 0g; Trans Fat 0g); Cholesterol 60mg; Sodium 350mg; Total Carbohydrate 16g (Dietary Fiber 1g) **% Daily Value:** Vitamin A 2%; Vitamin C 4%; Calcium 2%; Iron 4% **Exchanges:** 1 Starch, 3 Very Lean Meat **Carbohydrate Choices:** 1

Health experts recommend eating fish at least twice a week because it is an excellent source of protein and low in saturated fat.

Squash with Vegetarian Sausage and Rice Stuffing

Prep Time: 25 Minutes

Start to Finish: 25 Minutes

2 servings

1 medium acorn squash

½ cup frozen sweet peas

½ cup water

¼ teaspoon dried thyme leaves

⅛ teaspoon salt

½ cup uncooked instant brown rice

3 frozen soy-protein breakfast sausage links (from 8-oz box)

2 tablespoons shredded fresh Parmesan cheese

1 Cut squash in half lengthwise; remove seeds. In 8-inch square (2-quart) glass baking dish, place squash halves, cut side down. Cover with microwavable plastic wrap. Microwave on High 9 to 11 minutes or until squash is fork-tender.

2 Meanwhile, in 2-quart saucepan, heat peas, water, thyme and salt to boiling over high heat. Stir in rice; return to boiling. Reduce heat to low; cover and simmer 5 minutes. Remove from heat; stir. Let stand covered 5 minutes or until liquid is absorbed.

3 Heat 8-inch nonstick skillet over medium heat. Add sausage patties; cook 5 to 6 minutes or until lightly browned and hot, breaking up patties into ½-inch pieces as they thaw.

4 Fluff rice mixture with fork; stir in sausage links and cheese. Spoon rice mixture into squash halves.

1 Serving: Calories 360 (Calories from Fat 70); Total Fat 8g (Saturated Fat 2g; Trans Fat 0g); Cholesterol 0mg; Sodium 590mg; Total Carbohydrate 52g (Dietary Fiber 9g) **% Daily Value:** Vitamin A 25%; Vitamin C 15%; Calcium 20%; Iron 20% **Exchanges:** 3 Starch, ½ Other Carbohydrate, 1½ Lean Meat **Carbohydrate Choices:** 3½

By choosing meatless sausage, you can save about half the fat grams per patty compared with using pork or beef sausage.

Basil-Zucchini-Potato Frittata

Prep Time: 15 minutes

Start to Finish:
25 Minutes

4 servings

1 teaspoon olive or canola oil

½ cup medium red bell pepper, chopped (½ medium)

1 small onion, chopped (⅓ cup)

1 cup refrigerated shredded hash brown potatoes (from 20-oz bag)

1 medium zucchini, shredded (about 2 cups)

1 tablespoon water

3 whole eggs plus 3 egg whites, lightly beaten, or 1¼ cups fat-free cholesterol-free egg product (from two 8-oz cartons)

2 tablespoons chopped fresh basil or 1 teaspoon dried basil leaves

½ teaspoon garlic salt

1 cup reduced-fat tomato pasta sauce, heated

1 In 10-inch nonstick skillet, heat oil over medium-high heat. Add bell pepper and onion; cook 5 minutes, stirring frequently.

2 Reduce heat to medium. Add potatoes, zucchini and water; cover and cook 5 to 6 minutes, adding an additional 1 tablespoon water if necessary to prevent sticking, until vegetables are tender.

3 Meanwhile, in medium bowl, mix beaten eggs and egg whites, the basil and garlic salt until well blended.

4 Pour egg mixture over vegetables. Reduce heat to medium-low; cover and cook 7 to 10 minutes, lifting edges occasionally to allow uncooked egg mixture to flow to bottom of skillet, until egg mixture is set but still moist on top. Cut into wedges; serve topped with warm pasta sauce.

1 Serving: Calories 210 (Calories from Fat 70); Total Fat 7g (Saturated Fat 2g; Trans Fat 0g); Cholesterol 160mg; Sodium 530mg; Total Carbohydrate 27g (Dietary Fiber 3g) **% Daily Value:** Vitamin A 45%; Vitamin C 45%; Calcium 6%; Iron 8% **Exchanges:** 1½ Starch, 1 Very Lean Meat, 1 Fat **Carbohydrate Choices:** 2

A frittata is almost as quick to make as scrambled eggs and you can use leftover vegetables that you have on hand.

Colorful Veggie and Tortilla Dinner

Prep Time: 25 Minutes

Start to Finish:
25 Minutes

5 servings

¼ **cup water**

¼ **cup uncooked instant brown rice**

1½ **cups frozen mixed vegetables (from 1-lb bag), thawed**

2 **cans (14.5 oz each) no-salt-added stewed tomatoes, drained**

1 **can (15.5 oz) dark red kidney beans, drained, rinsed**

¼ **cup finely chopped fresh cilantro**

½ **medium onion, finely chopped (¼ cup)**

1 **teaspoon ground cumin**

1 **teaspoon ground coriander**

2 **large cloves garlic, finely chopped**

¼ **teaspoon pepper**

5 **fat-free flour tortillas (8 inch), heated**

¼ **cup fat-free sour cream**

Chopped fresh cilantro

2 **medium plum (Roma) tomatoes, chopped (⅔ cup)**

1   In 2-quart saucepan, heat water to boiling. Stir in rice; return to boiling. Reduce heat; cover and cook 5 to 10 minutes or until liquid is absorbed.

2   Stir in thawed vegetables, stewed tomatoes, beans, ¼ cup cilantro, the onion, cumin, coriander, garlic and pepper. Cook until hot.

3   Place warm tortillas on individual plates. Cover tortillas evenly with rice mixture. Top each with sour cream, chopped cilantro and tomatoes.

1 Serving: Calories 370 (Calories from Fat 15); Total Fat 1.5g (Saturated Fat 0g; Trans Fat 0g); Cholesterol 0mg; Sodium 520mg; Total Carbohydrate 72g (Dietary Fiber 12g) **% Daily Value:** Vitamin A 60%; Vitamin C 20%; Calcium 20%; Iron 35% **Exchanges:** 3 Starch, 1 Other Carbohydrate, 2 Vegetable, ½ Very Lean Meat **Carbohydrate Choices:** 5

Love meat but trying to cut down on the amount you eat? Try to make a meatless dinner at least once a week to reduce fat and calories.

meals in 20 minutes max

Sloppy Joe Confetti Tacos, see page 74

Chicken-Tortellini Soup

 **Superfast**

Prep Time: 20 Minutes

Start to Finish:
20 Minutes

4 servings (2 cups each)

2 cans (14 oz each) fat-free chicken broth with 33% less sodium

3 cups water

⅓ cup sliced green onions

½ teaspoon dried basil leaves

2 cloves garlic, finely chopped

½ lb precut chicken breast chunks or 2 boneless skinless chicken breasts (½ lb), cut into ½-inch pieces

1 package (9 oz) refrigerated cheese-filled tortellini

1 cup chopped fresh spinach

1 cup frozen sweet peas

1   In 3-quart saucepan or Dutch oven, heat broth, water, onions, basil and garlic to boiling. Stir in chicken and tortellini. Reduce heat to medium; simmer uncovered 4 minutes.

2   Add spinach and peas; cook 5 minutes, stirring occasionally, until spinach is wilted, tortellini is tender and chicken is no longer pink in center. If desired, season to taste with pepper.

1 Serving: Calories 330 (Calories from Fat 60); Total Fat 7g (Saturated Fat 3g; Trans Fat 0g); Cholesterol 70mg; Sodium 750mg; Total Carbohydrate 37g (Dietary Fiber 3g) **% Daily Value:** Vitamin A 30%; Vitamin C 6%; Calcium 10%; Iron 15% **Exchanges:** 2 Starch, ½ Other Carbohydrate, 3 Very Lean Meat, 1 Fat **Carbohydrate Choices:** 2½

Rush-Hour Chili

 **Superfast**

Prep Time: 20 Minutes

Start to Finish: 20 Minutes

4 servings (1¼ cups each)

¾ lb extra-lean (at least 90%) ground beef

1 can (15.5 or 15 oz) kidney beans, drained, rinsed

1 can (14.5 oz) diced tomatoes, undrained

1 can (6 oz) tomato paste

2 cups cold water

2 teaspoons chili powder

1 In 3-quart nonstick saucepan or Dutch oven, cook beef over medium-high heat 5 to 7 minutes, stirring frequently, until thoroughly cooked; drain if necessary.

2 Stir in remaining ingredients. Heat to boiling. Reduce heat to medium-low; cover and simmer 5 to 7 minutes, stirring occasionally, until hot.

1 Serving: Calories 310 (Calories from Fat 70); Total Fat 8g (Saturated Fat 3g; Trans Fat 0g); Cholesterol 55mg; Sodium 530mg; Total Carbohydrate 34g (Dietary Fiber 9g) **% Daily Value:** Vitamin A 25%; Vitamin C 15%; Calcium 10%; Iron 35% **Exchanges:** 1 Starch, 1 Other Carbohydrate, 1 Vegetable, 3 Very Lean Meat, 1 Fat **Carbohydrate Choices:** 2

one bean for another

Bean choices in recipes are often based on ethnic traditions, but that doesn't mean you can't use a different bean. Beans are fairly interchangeable, so follow your own tastes or use what you have on hand when choosing which bean to cook with.

tips for freezing soup

Many soups freeze well, giving you a ready arsenal of homemade last-minute suppers or lunches.

- Freeze soups in individual portions for flexibility, unless you're sure you'll be feeding a crowd.
- When using glass containers, select only those that are recommended for the freezer, such as canning jars. Other glass containers could shatter when food freezes and expands.
- Label containers with waterproof marker on freezer tape, adhesive labels or tie-on labels. Include the name of the soup and the date it was prepared.
- Most soups will retain best color, flavor and texture if frozen for less than four to six weeks.
- Seal loose-fitting lids with freezer tape, which sticks better in cold temperatures than masking tape.
- Use a freezer thermometer to make sure the temperature stays at 0°F.
- Liquids expand as they freeze, so leave half inch empty at the top of the container.
- For a single portion, microwave reheating is convenient. Since multiple servings take proportionately longer in the microwave, heat larger batches on the stovetop.

Minestrone Salad

 **Superfast**

Prep Time: 20 Minutes

Start to Finish:
20 Minutes

12 servings

5 cups uncooked bow-tie
(farfalle) pasta (10 oz)

1 can (15.5 or 15 oz) red
kidney beans, drained, rinsed

1 package (3.5 oz) sliced
pepperoni

4 plum (Roma) tomatoes,
coarsely chopped

½ cup chopped green bell
pepper

¼ cup chopped fresh parsley

¼ cup freshly shredded
Parmesan cheese (1 oz)

Freshly ground black pepper,
if desired

1 bottle (8 oz) fat-free Italian
dressing

1 Cook and drain pasta as directed on package. Rinse with cold water to cool.

2 In large bowl, mix cooked pasta and remaining ingredients. Serve immediately, or cover and refrigerate until serving time.

1 Serving: Calories 200 (Calories from Fat 45); Total Fat 5g (Saturated Fat 2g; Trans Fat 0g); Cholesterol 10mg; Sodium 490mg; Total Carbohydrate 30g (Dietary Fiber 3g) **% Daily Value:** Vitamin A 6%; Vitamin C 15%; Calcium 6%; Iron 10% **Exchanges:** 2 Starch, ½ Lean Meat, ½ Fat **Carbohydrate Choices:** 2

Any medium-size pasta can be used in place of the bow-tie pasta.

salad shortcuts

- Slice carrots, celery and radishes to use over several days. Wrap cut vegetables in a damp paper towel and refrigerate in a self-seal plastic bag.

- Extend salads and add a novel touch with canned ingredients from your pantry. Water chestnuts, pineapple chunks, olives, artichoke hearts, pickles and baby corn are good choices.

- Transform the humble can of tuna into an easy gourmet delight by adding chopped red onion, carrot, cucumber and other veggies in season.

- Use up leftovers. Cooked potatoes, grilled chicken, steamed green beans and corn on the cob are just a few ingredients that gracefully make the switch from last night's star to tonight's supporting role in a salad.

- When cooking rice or pasta, cook more than you need and the rest tomorrow in a cool salad that doesn't even require you water.

- Buy coleslaw mix instead of shredding all that cabbage for coleslaw.

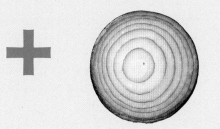

Pan-Seared Sirloin Steak  Superfast

Prep Time: 15 Minutes

Start to Finish:
15 Minutes

4 servings

1 lb boneless beef sirloin
steak, 1 inch thick

¾ teaspoon lemon-pepper
seasoning

1 tablespoon grated lemon
peel

1 tablespoon soy sauce

2 tablespoons olive oil

1 Sprinkle beef with lemon-pepper seasoning. In small bowl, mix lemon peel, soy sauce and 1 tablespoon of the oil; brush over both sides of beef.

2 In 10-inch nonstick skillet, heat remaining tablespoon oil over medium heat until hot. Add beef; cook 10 to 12 minutes or until browned on both sides and desired doneness. Cut into 4 serving pieces.

1 Serving: Calories 220 (Calories from Fat 100); Total Fat 11g (Saturated Fat 2.5g; Trans Fat 0g); Cholesterol 75mg; Sodium 400mg; Total Carbohydrate 0g (Dietary Fiber 0g) **% Daily Value:** Vitamin A 0%; Vitamin C 0%; Calcium 0%; Iron 15% **Exchanges:** 4 Lean Meat **Carbohydrate Choices:** 0

meat tips for the hurried cook

- For faster cooking, choose thin, boneless cuts, such as boneless pork chops, thin steaks, slices of lamb leg or pork tenderloin.

- Ground meat cooks quickly and is very versatile, but can be high in fat. Look for packages marked "extra lean" or choose a chunk of lean meat and ask the butcher to grind it for you. You'll probably pay a little more, but you will be paying for meat, not fat.

- Speed up cooking by cutting meat into strips or cubes. Many supermarkets sell strips or chunks of meat packaged for stewing or stir-frying.

To complete the meal, serve the steak with au gratin potatoes and an Italian salad from the deli.

Sloppy Joe Confetti Tacos

 **Superfast**

See photo, page 64

Prep Time: 20 Minutes

Start to Finish:
20 Minutes

6 servings (2 tacos each)

1 lb extra-lean (at least 90%) ground beef

1 box (4.6 oz) taco shells (12 shells)

1 can (15.5 oz) sloppy joe sauce

1 small red bell pepper, chopped

1 can (11 oz) whole kernel sweet corn, drained

1 can (2¼ oz) sliced ripe olives, drained

1 cup thinly sliced romaine lettuce

¼ cup shredded mozzarella cheese (1 oz)

¼ cup shredded reduced-fat sharp Cheddar cheese (1 oz)

1 Heat oven to 350°F. In 10-inch skillet, cook beef over medium-high heat 5 to 7 minutes, stirring frequently, until thoroughly cooked; drain if necessary.

2 Meanwhile, heat taco shells as directed on box.

3 Stir sloppy joe sauce, bell pepper and corn into beef. Cook 2 to 3 minutes longer, stirring occasionally, until mixture is hot and bubbly.

4 Spoon about ¼ cup beef mixture into each warm taco shell; top with olives, lettuce and cheeses.

1 Serving: Calories 330 (Calories from Fat 120); Total Fat 13g (Saturated Fat 4.5g; Trans Fat 1.5g); Cholesterol 50mg; Sodium 850mg; Total Carbohydrate 31g (Dietary Fiber 4g) **% Daily Value:** Vitamin A 25%; Vitamin C 15%; Calcium 10%; Iron 20% **Exchanges:** 1½ Starch, ½ Other Carbohydrate, 2 Medium-Fat Meat, ½ Fat **Carbohydrate Choices:** 2

Use taco shells with flat bottoms for easier filling and a little extra room.

Chili-Lime Pork Chops

 Superfast

Prep Time: 15 Minutes

Start to Finish:
15 Minutes

4 servings

SEASONING

1 teaspoon chili powder

½ teaspoon garlic salt

⅛ teaspoon ground red pepper (cayenne)

1 tablespoon lime juice

1 teaspoon canola oil

PORK

4 boneless pork loin chops, ½ to ¾ inch thick (1 lb)

IF DESIRED

Chopped fresh cilantro

Lime wedges

1 Heat closed contact grill for 5 minutes.

2 Meanwhile, in small bowl, mix all seasoning ingredients. Brush mixture evenly on both sides of each pork chop.

3 When grill is heated, place pork chops on bottom grill surface. Close grill; cook 5 to 7 minutes or until pork is no longer pink in center. Sprinkle pork with cilantro and serve with lime wedges.

1 Serving: Calories 190 (Calories from Fat 90); Total Fat 10g (Saturated Fat 3g; Trans Fat 0g); Cholesterol 70mg; Sodium 170mg; Total Carbohydrate 0g (Dietary Fiber 0g) **% Daily Value:** Vitamin A 4%; Vitamin C 0%; Calcium 0%; Iron 6% **Exchanges:** 3½ Lean Meat **Carbohydrate Choices:** 0

turn up the heat

Pepper is a highly personal matter. While a few people find even ordinary black pepper overpowering, there's a growing legion of fire-breathers who relish foods bearing labels such as: "Shake well and good luck." In between there's a continuum of peppers, ranging from flavorful but mild to incendiary. Some of the hot ways you can add zing to dips and other appetizers:

Paprika: Made from ground chile peppers, paprika may be either mild "sweet" or "hot." A sprinkle of the sweet variety makes a colorful garnish.

Pure ground chile: As opposed to chili powder, which is a blend of spices, pure ground chile contains nothing but chile peppers. Varieties range from mild to hot.

Pork and Pineapple Stir-Fry  Superfast

Prep Time: 20 Minutes
Start to Finish:
20 Minutes
4 servings (1¾ cups each)

1¼ cups uncooked instant rice

1¾ cups water

4 tablespoons packed brown sugar

1½ teaspoons cornstarch

½ teaspoon ground ginger

¼ teaspoon crushed red pepper flakes, if desired

3 tablespoons soy sauce

1 can (20 oz) pineapple chunks or 16 fresh pineapple chunks, drained, 2 tablespoons liquid reserved

¾ lb boneless lean pork, cut into thin bite-size strips

1 bag (16 oz) coleslaw mix (shredded cabbage and carrots)

1 Cook rice in 1¼ cups of the water as directed on package.

2 Meanwhile, in small bowl, mix 3 tablespoons of the brown sugar, the cornstarch, ginger, pepper flakes, the remaining ½ cup water, the soy sauce and reserved 2 tablespoons pineapple liquid; set aside.

3 Heat 12-inch nonstick skillet over medium-high heat. Add drained pineapple chunks; sprinkle with remaining 1 tablespoon brown sugar. Cook 5 minutes, turning chunks occasionally.

4 Remove pineapple from skillet; set aside. In same skillet, cook and stir pork over medium-high heat 2 minutes.

5 Add coleslaw mix; cook and stir 3 to 6 minutes or until pork is no longer pink in center and cabbage is tender.

6 Stir pineapple and cornstarch mixture into pork mixture; cook and stir about 3 minutes or until pork is glazed and sauce is slightly thickened. Serve over rice.

1 Serving: Calories 440 (Calories from Fat 70); Total Fat 7g (Saturated Fat 2.5g; Trans Fat 0g); Cholesterol 55mg; Sodium 750mg; Total Carbohydrate 69g (Dietary Fiber 5g) **% Daily Value:** Vitamin A 70%; Vitamin C 40%; Calcium 10%; Iron 20% **Exchanges:** 1 Starch, 1 Fruit, 2 Other Carbohydrate, 1½ Vegetable, 2½ Lean Meat **Carbohydrate Choices:** 4½

Orange-Zested Chicken Breasts

 **Superfast**

Prep Time: 20 Minutes

Start to Finish:
20 Minutes

4 servings

½ **teaspoon seasoned salt**

¼ **teaspoon garlic powder**

1 **tablespoon canola oil**

1 **teaspoon grated orange peel**

4 **boneless skinless chicken breasts (1 lb)**

1 In small bowl, mix seasoned salt and garlic powder.

2 In 10-inch nonstick skillet, heat oil and orange peel over medium heat. Add chicken; sprinkle with salt mixture. Cook about 15 minutes, turning once, until juice of chicken is clear when center of thickest part is cut (170°F).

1 Serving: Calories 160 (Calories from Fat 60); Total Fat 7g (Saturated Fat 1.5g; Trans Fat 0g); Cholesterol 70mg; Sodium 230mg; Total Carbohydrate 0g (Dietary Fiber 0g) **% Daily Value:** Vitamin A 0%; Vitamin C 0%; Calcium 0%; Iron 4% **Exchanges:** 3½ Very Lean Meat, 1 Fat **Carbohydrate Choices:** 0

This orange chicken is super easy to prepare! Serve it with cooked fresh green beans or broccoli, warm breadsticks and a simple fruit salad.

chicken storage and safety

- At the supermarket, check the "sell-by" date on the package and plan to use it within two days (one is better), regardless of the freshness date on the package.

- Bring chicken directly home from the market and store it in the coldest part of the refrigerator. Set the package on a plate to catch any drips.

- Refrigerate chicken in its original wrapper; if torn, overwrap it with plastic.

- Scrub your hands before and after handling raw chicken.

- Use hot, soapy water to wash knives, cutting boards and anything else that has come into contact with raw chicken.

- For best quality, use whole frozen chicken within one year, parts within nine months and giblets or ground meat within four months.

- Although freezer burn is unpleasant, it is not dangerous. Use a sharp knife to cut away any discolored areas.

- Cook chicken until the juices run clear and no trace of pink remains.

- Put food away as soon as possible after the meal, but definitely within two hours. Cooked leftover chicken can be refrigerated for three to four days.

- Frozen leftovers will be best if used within three to six months. Longer freezing will not affect safety, but the flavor, texture and color qualities may deteriorate.

Easy Chicken Tetrazzini  Superfast

Prep Time: 20 Minutes

Start to Finish:
20 Minutes

4 servings (1¼ cups each)

1 package (7 oz) spaghetti,
broken into thirds

1 tablespoon butter or
margarine

8 medium green onions,
sliced (½ cup)

1 package (8 oz) sliced fresh
mushrooms (3 cups)

3 tablespoons all-purpose
flour

¼ teaspoon garlic powder

⅛ teaspoon pepper

1 cup chicken broth

½ cup fat-free (skim) milk

2 cups cubed cooked chicken

1 jar (2 oz) sliced pimientos,
drained

2 tablespoons dry sherry, if
desired

¼ cup grated Parmesan
cheese

1 In 3-quart saucepan, cook and drain spaghetti as directed on package; set aside.

2 In same saucepan, melt butter over medium-high heat. Add onions and mushrooms; cook, stirring frequently, until tender. In small bowl, mix flour, garlic powder, pepper, broth and milk until smooth. Gradually stir into onion mixture, cooking and stirring until bubbly and thickened.

3 Stir in chicken, pimientos and sherry. Cook, stirring occasionally, until hot. Stir in cheese. Add cooked spaghetti; toss gently. If desired, serve with additional grated Parmesan cheese and chopped fresh parsley.

1 Serving: Calories 460 (Calories from Fat 110); Total Fat 12g (Saturated Fat 5g; Trans Fat 0g); Cholesterol 75mg; Sodium 670mg; Total Carbohydrate 53g (Dietary Fiber 4g) **% Daily Value:** Vitamin A 15%; Vitamin C 15%; Calcium 15%; Iron 20% **Exchanges:** 2½ Starch, ½ Other Carbohydrate, 1 Vegetable, 3½ Lean Meat **Carbohydrate Choices:** 3½

Vermicelli with Fresh Herb-Tomato Sauce

 **Superfast**

Prep Time: 20 Minutes
Start to Finish:
20 Minutes
5 servings (1¼ cups each)

1 package (7 oz) vermicelli

3 medium tomatoes, seeded, chopped (about 2 cups)

½ cup shredded Parmesan cheese (2 oz)

2 tablespoons chopped fresh basil leaves

2 tablespoons chopped fresh chives

2 tablespoons olive oil

½ teaspoon salt

½ teaspoon finely grated lemon peel

⅛ teaspoon coarse ground black pepper

1 clove garlic, finely chopped

1 Cook and drain vermicelli as directed on package.

2 Meanwhile, in large bowl, mix remaining ingredients.

3 Gently stir cooked vermicelli into tomato mixture to coat.

1 Serving: Calories 280 (Calories from Fat 90); Total Fat 10g (Saturated Fat 3g; Trans Fat 0g); Cholesterol 10mg; Sodium 580mg; Total Carbohydrate 38g (Dietary Fiber 3g) **% Daily Value:** Vitamin A 15%; Vitamin C 8%; Calcium 15%; Iron 10% **Exchanges:** 2 Starch, 1 Vegetable, 2 Fat **Carbohydrate Choices:** 2½

To chop fresh herbs, place them in a glass measuring cup, and snip them with kitchen scissors in the cup.

Salmon with Lemon Butter and Pineapple Salsa

 Superfast

Prep Time: 10 Minutes

Start to Finish: 20 Minutes

4 servings

LEMON BUTTER

1 tablespoon butter or margarine, softened

4 teaspoons grated lemon peel

2 teaspoons lemon juice

PINEAPPLE SALSA

2 cups chopped fresh pineapple

¼ cup chopped fresh cilantro

2 tablespoons finely chopped red onion

1 teaspoon finely chopped jalapeño chile, if desired

SALMON

4 salmon fillets, about 1 inch thick (1½ lb)

¼ teaspoon salt

1 Heat oven to 375°F. In small bowl, mix lemon butter ingredients; set aside.

2 In medium bowl, mix pineapple salsa ingredients; cover and refrigerate until serving time.

3 Line 13×9-inch pan with foil. Place salmon, skin side down, in pan; sprinkle with salt.

4 Bake 8 to 10 minutes or until fish flakes easily with fork. Immediately top salmon with lemon butter. Serve with pineapple salsa.

1 Serving: Calories 300 (Calories from Fat 110); Total Fat 13g (Saturated Fat 4.5g; Trans Fat 0g); Cholesterol 120mg; Sodium 270mg; Total Carbohydrate 11g (Dietary Fiber 1g) **% Daily Value:** Vitamin A 8%; Vitamin C 30%; Calcium 4%; Iron 8% **Exchanges:** ½ Fruit, 5 Lean Meat **Carbohydrate Choices:** 1

If you prefer halibut, go ahead and substitute it for the salmon. Just follow the guidelines for the thickness and weight called for in the recipe.

Fish Fillets with Herbed Tartar Sauce

 **Superfast**

Prep Time: 20 Minutes
Start to Finish:
20 Minutes
4 servings

1 egg

½ cup Italian-style dry bread crumbs

1 tablespoon olive oil

1 lb mild-flavored fish fillets (about ½ inch thick), cut into 4 serving pieces

⅓ cup fat-free tartar sauce

¼ cup chopped tomato

½ teaspoon dried basil leaves

1 In shallow dish, beat egg with wire whisk. In another shallow dish, place bread crumbs.

2 In 12-inch nonstick skillet, heat oil over medium heat until hot. Dip fish into egg, then coat with bread crumbs; place in skillet. Cook 8 to 10 minutes, turning once, until browned on both sides and fish flakes easily with fork.

3 In small bowl, mix tartar sauce, tomato and basil; serve with fish.

1 Serving: Calories 220 (Calories from Fat 60); Total Fat 7g (Saturated Fat 1.5g; Trans Fat 0g); Cholesterol 115mg; Sodium 470mg; Total Carbohydrate 14g (Dietary Fiber 0g) **% Daily Value:** Vitamin A 4%; Vitamin C 0%; Calcium 4%; Iron 6% **Exchanges:** 1 Starch, 3 Very Lean Meat, 1 Fat **Carbohydrate Choices:** 1

Fish that would work well in this recipe include cod, walleye, perch, sole or any other mild-flavored fillets.

Couscous-Stuffed Red Bell Peppers

 **Superfast**

Prep Time: 20 Minutes

Start to Finish: 20 Minutes

2 servings (2 pepper halves each)

1 box (5.7 oz) roasted garlic and olive oil-flavored couscous mix

1¼ cups water

2 large red bell peppers, cut in half lengthwise, seeds and membranes removed

1 cup chopped fresh spinach

¼ cup grated Parmesan cheese

1 Cook couscous in water as directed on box, omitting oil; cover to keep warm.

2 Meanwhile, in 8-inch square (2-quart) microwavable dish, arrange bell pepper halves; add 2 tablespoons water. Cover with microwavable waxed paper. Microwave on High 3 to 4 minutes or just until crisp-tender.

3 Stir spinach and cheese into couscous. Spoon mixture into pepper halves.

1 Serving: Calories 400 (Calories from Fat 60); Total Fat 6g (Saturated Fat 2.5g; Trans Fat 0g); Cholesterol 10mg; Sodium 1030mg; Total Carbohydrate 70g (Dietary Fiber 6g) **% Daily Value:** Vitamin A 130%; Vitamin C 180%; Calcium 15%; Iron 15% **Exchanges:** 4 Starch, 2 Vegetable, ½ Fat **Carbohydrate Choices:** 4½

about couscous

Couscous resembles a grain but is actually a tiny pasta that's very popular in Middle Eastern cooking. Its mild flavor makes it a good complement to a variety of savory dishes, and the quick-cooking version found in most supermarkets takes only five minutes to prepare.

Looking for quick and easy recipes served in a different way? No need to precook the peppers in this recipe!

Scrambled Egg and Veggie Pockets

 Superfast

Prep Time: 20 Minutes

Start to Finish:
20 Minutes

4 sandwiches

1 carton (8 oz) fat-free egg product (1 cup) or 4 eggs, lightly beaten

½ cup shredded American cheese (2 oz)

½ teaspoon onion powder

1 tablespoon butter or margarine

1 cup chopped broccoli

½ cup shredded carrot

¼ cup chopped red or green bell pepper

2 tablespoons sliced ripe olives

2 pita (pocket) breads (6 inch), cut in half to form pockets

1 In medium bowl, mix egg product, cheese and onion powder; set aside.

2 In 10-inch skillet, melt butter over medium heat. Add broccoli, carrot, bell pepper and olives; cook 3 to 5 minutes, stirring frequently, until vegetables are crisp-tender.

3 Pour egg mixture over vegetables; reduce heat to low. Cook, stirring occasionally from outside edge to center, allowing uncooked egg mixture to flow to bottom of skillet, until center is set but still moist.

4 Spoon egg mixture evenly into pita bread halves.

1 Sandwich: Calories 200 (Calories from Fat 70); Total Fat 8g (Saturated Fat 4.5g; Trans Fat 0g); Cholesterol 20mg; Sodium 530mg; Total Carbohydrate 19g (Dietary Fiber 2g) **% Daily Value:** Vitamin A 70%; Vitamin C 30%; Calcium 15%; Iron 10% **Exchanges:** 1 Starch, 1 Vegetable, 1 Lean Meat, 1 Fat **Carbohydrate Choices:** 1

The veggies add lots of crunch and lots of vitamins and minerals to this easy, colorful dinner. Use your family's favorites or any veggies on hand.

Olé Salsa Potatoes

 **Superfast**

Prep Time: 20 Minutes

Start to Finish:
20 Minutes

4 servings (2 potato halves each)

4 large baking potatoes (about 8 oz each)

1 lb extra-lean (at least 90%) ground beef

½ cup chunky-style salsa

1 teaspoon chili powder

½ cup shredded reduced-fat sharp Cheddar cheese (2 oz)

Sour cream, if desired

Additional salsa, if desired

1 Pierce potatoes several times with fork. Place on microwavable paper towel in microwave oven. Microwave on High 10 to 13 minutes or until tender, turning potatoes over and rearranging halfway through cooking. Let stand in microwave oven 5 minutes.

2 Meanwhile, in 10-inch nonstick skillet, cook beef over medium-high heat 5 to 7 minutes, stirring frequently, until thoroughly cooked; drain if necessary. Stir in ½ cup salsa and the chili powder.

3 Cut potatoes in half lengthwise; place 2 halves on each plate. Spoon beef mixture evenly over potatoes. Sprinkle 2 tablespoons cheese over each serving. Serve with sour cream and additional salsa.

1 Serving: Calories 380 (Calories from Fat 90); Total Fat 10g (Saturated Fat 4.5g; Trans Fat 0.5g); Cholesterol 75mg; Sodium 400mg; Total Carbohydrate 41g (Dietary Fiber 5g) **% Daily Value:** Vitamin A 6%; Vitamin C 15%; Calcium 15%; Iron 25% **Exchanges:** 2 Starch, ½ Other Carbohydrate, 3½ Lean Meat **Carbohydrate Choices:** 3

Lightly press down and roll each "baked" potato on the kitchen counter before cutting it in half. This softens the flesh of the potato and makes it easier to eat.

Fast Fajita and Vegetable Pita ◗ Superfast

Prep Time: 10 Minutes

Start to Finish:
10 Minutes

6 sandwiches

¼ **cup fat-free Italian dressing**

2 to 3 teaspoons lime juice

½ **lb thinly sliced, cooked roast beef, cut into strips (2 cups)**

½ **cup chopped fresh broccoli**

1 small tomato, chopped (½ cup)

3 pita (pocket) breads (6 inch), cut in half to form pockets

6 leaves lettuce

1 In medium bowl, mix dressing and lime juice. Add roast beef, broccoli and tomato; toss to coat.

2 To serve, line pita bread halves with lettuce. Fill each with about ½ cup beef mixture. If desired, drizzle with additional Italian dressing.

1 Sandwich: Calories 170 (Calories from Fat 60); Total Fat 6g (Saturated Fat 2.5g; Trans Fat 0g); Cholesterol 30mg; Sodium 280mg; Total Carbohydrate 16g (Dietary Fiber 1g) **% Daily Value:** Vitamin A 10%; Vitamin C 8%; Calcium 4%; Iron 10% **Exchanges:** 1 Starch, 1½ Lean Meat **Carbohydrate Choices:** 1

tomatoes and your health

Lycopene, found in tomatoes and processed tomato products, is an antioxidant that may reduce the risk of certain types of cancer, including prostate cancer. Cooked tomatoes may be particularly beneficial because heat appears to increase the amount of lycopene absorbed by the body.

fast family favorites

chapter

4

Spicy Mexican Cheese Chowder, see page 97

Smoked Turkey–Potato Chowder

Prep Time: 30 Minutes
Start to Finish:
30 Minutes
4 servings (1½ cups each)

1 tablespoon butter or margarine

1 cup sliced celery (2 medium stalks)

2 tablespoons all-purpose flour

⅛ teaspoon pepper

1 can (14 oz) fat-free chicken broth with 33% less sodium

3 cups frozen potatoes O'Brien with onions and peppers (from 28-oz bag)

6 oz smoked turkey breast, cut into cubes (1⅓ cups)

1 cup frozen sweet peas

2 cups fat-free (skim) milk

¼ cup chopped fresh parsley

1 In 3-quart saucepan, melt butter over medium heat. Add celery; cook 2 to 3 minutes, stirring frequently, until crisp-tender.

2 Stir in flour and pepper until well blended. Increase heat to medium-high; gradually stir in broth, cooking and stirring until bubbly and thickened.

3 Stir in potatoes, turkey breast, peas and milk. Heat to boiling. Reduce heat to low; cover and simmer 8 to 10 minutes, stirring occasionally, until potatoes are tender. Stir in parsley during last 2 minutes of cook time.

1 Serving: Calories 240 (Calories from Fat 35); Total Fat 3.5g (Saturated Fat 2g; Trans Fat 0g); Cholesterol 45mg; Sodium 390mg; Total Carbohydrate 29g (Dietary Fiber 3g) **% Daily Value:** Vitamin A 30%; Vitamin C 10%; Calcium 20%; Iron 10% **Exchanges:** 1 Starch, ½ Skim Milk, 1 Vegetable, 1½ Lean Meat **Carbohydrate Choices:** 2

Light Chicken–Wild Rice Soup

 **Superfast**

Prep Time: 20 Minutes

Start to Finish:
20 Minutes

6 servings (1½ cups each)

4 slices bacon

3 boneless skinless chicken breasts, cut into ¾-inch pieces

1 box (6.2 oz) fast-cooking long-grain and wild rice mix (with seasoning packet)

2 cans (14 oz each) fat-free chicken broth with 33% less sodium

4 cups fat-free (skim) milk

¾ cup all-purpose flour

1½ teaspoons diced pimientos

1 tablespoon dry sherry, if desired

1 Cook bacon until crisp. Drain on paper towel; crumble and set aside.

2 In nonstick Dutch oven or 4-quart saucepan, mix chicken, rice with contents of seasoning packet and broth. Heat to boiling. Reduce heat to low; cover and simmer 5 to 10 minutes or until rice is tender.

3 In small jar with tight-fitting lid, shake 1 cup of the milk and the flour until well blended.

4 Add flour mixture, remaining 3 cups milk, the bacon, pimientos and sherry to rice mixture; cook over medium heat, stirring constantly, until soup is bubbly and thickened and chicken is no longer pink in center. If desired, season to taste with salt and pepper.

1 Serving: Calories 320 (Calories from Fat 45); Total Fat 5g (Saturated Fat 1.5g; Trans Fat 0g); Cholesterol 45mg; Sodium 910mg; Total Carbohydrate 42g (Dietary Fiber 1g) **% Daily Value:** Vitamin A 8%; Vitamin C 2%; Calcium 25%; Iron 15% **Exchanges:** 2 Starch, ½ Other Carbohydrate, ½ Skim Milk, 2½ Very Lean Meat **Carbohydrate Choices:** 3

Spicy Mexican Cheese Chowder

 **Superfast**

See photo, page 92

Prep Time: 20 Minutes

Start to Finish:
20 Minutes

3 servings (1½ cups each)

1 can (14 oz) fat-free chicken broth with 33% less sodium

1 bag (1 lb) frozen broccoli, carrots and cauliflower

1 cup fat-free (skim) milk

2 tablespoons cornstarch

4 oz Mexican prepared cheese product with jalapeño peppers (from 16-oz loaf), cut into cubes

1 In 3-quart saucepan, heat broth to boiling over high heat. Stir in frozen vegetables. Return to boiling. Reduce heat; cover and simmer 5 minutes.

2 Meanwhile, in small bowl, mix milk and cornstarch until smooth.

3 Stir cornstarch mixture into vegetable mixture, cooking and stirring until thickened. Remove from heat. Stir in cheese until melted. If desired, sprinkle with freshly ground black pepper.

1 Serving: Calories 210 (Calories from Fat 70); Total Fat 8g (Saturated Fat 5g; Trans Fat 0g); Cholesterol 25mg; Sodium 810mg; Total Carbohydrate 20g (Dietary Fiber 4g) **% Daily Value:** Vitamin A 70%; Vitamin C 40%; Calcium 35%; Iron 8% **Exchanges:** 1 Other Carbohydrate, 1½ Vegetable, 1½ Medium-Fat Meat **Carbohydrate Choices:** 1

You can turn down the heat by using cheese without the peppers in this quick and hearty chowder.

Vegetable-Beef-Barley Soup

Prep Time: 30 Minutes

Start to Finish:
30 Minutes

4 servings (1½ cups each)

½ lb extra-lean (at least 90%) ground beef

1 cup frozen mixed vegetables

⅓ cup uncooked quick-cooking barley

1 can (14.5 oz) stewed tomatoes, undrained, cut up

1 can (14 oz) beef broth

1 can (8 oz) no-salt-added tomato sauce

1 In 3-quart saucepan, cook beef over medium-high heat 5 to 7 minutes, stirring frequently, until thoroughly cooked; drain if necessary.

2 Stir in remaining ingredients. Heat to boiling. Reduce heat to medium; cover and cook 10 to 15 minutes, stirring occasionally, until vegetables and barley are tender.

1 Serving: Calories 230 (Calories from Fat 45); Total Fat 5g (Saturated Fat 2g; Trans Fat 0g); Cholesterol 35mg; Sodium 770mg; Total Carbohydrate 30g (Dietary Fiber 6g) **% Daily Value:** Vitamin A 45%; Vitamin C 15%; Calcium 6%; Iron 20% **Exchanges:** 1 Starch, ½ Other Carbohydrate, 1 Vegetable, 1½ Lean Meat **Carbohydrate Choices:** 2

Barley can be found near the rice at your supermarket. Be sure to purchase the quick-cooking kind for this soup or it won't be tender in the 15 minutes cooking time.

Curried Pumpkin-Vegetable Soup

 **Superfast**

Prep Time: 20 Minutes

Start to Finish:
20 Minutes

4 servings (1½ cups each)

1 teaspoon olive oil

1 medium onion, chopped
(½ cup)

1 clove garlic, finely chopped

2 cups frozen mixed
vegetables

1 can (15 oz) pumpkin (not
pumpkin pie mix)

1 can (14.5 oz) diced
tomatoes, undrained

1 can (14 oz) fat-free chicken
broth with 33% less sodium

½ cup water

½ teaspoon sugar

1½ teaspoons curry powder

1 teaspoon paprika

1 In 3-quart saucepan, heat oil over medium-high heat. Add onion and garlic; cook 1 to 2 minutes, stirring frequently, until onion is crisp-tender.

2 Stir in remaining ingredients. Heat to boiling. Reduce heat to low; cover and simmer 10 to 12 minutes, stirring occasionally, until vegetables are tender. If desired, season to taste with pepper.

1 Serving: Calories 160 (Calories from Fat 15); Total Fat 2g (Saturated Fat 0g; Trans Fat 0g); Cholesterol 0mg; Sodium 420mg; Total Carbohydrate 28g (Dietary Fiber 9g) **% Daily Value:** Vitamin A 420%; Vitamin C 15%; Calcium 10%; Iron 20% **Exchanges:** 1 Starch, 2 Vegetable, ½ Fat **Carbohydrate Choices:** 2

Pumpkin is an excellent source of vitamin A. This nutrient is important for night vision and maintaining healthy skin.

Foot-Long Pizza

Prep Time: 30 Minutes
Start to Finish: 30 Minutes
4 servings

1 loaf (12 inch) French bread, cut in half lengthwise

¼ cup garlic-and-herbs spreadable cheese (from 4- to 6.5-oz container)

1 cup thinly sliced mushrooms

1 cup thin strips red, green or yellow bell pepper

½ cup julienne (matchstick-cut) zucchini (2×¼×¼ inch)

⅓ cup sliced ripe olives

Olive oil cooking spray or regular cooking spray

1 teaspoon Italian seasoning

½ cup shredded reduced-fat mozzarella cheese (2 oz)

1 Heat oven to 450°F. Line 15×10×1-inch pan with foil. Place bread halves, cut side up, in pan.

2 Spread spreadable cheese evenly over each bread half. Arrange mushrooms, bell pepper, zucchini and olives evenly over top. Spray gently with cooking spray. Sprinkle with Italian seasoning.

3 Bake about 15 minutes or just until vegetables begin to brown. Reduce oven temperature to 425°F. Sprinkle cheese over pizza.

4 Bake at 425°F about 5 minutes longer or until cheese is melted. Cut each bread half in half crosswise. Wrap each serving securely with foil; take with you for an on-the-go dinner.

1 Serving: Calories 330 (Calories from Fat 110); Total Fat 12g (Saturated Fat 6g; Trans Fat 0g); Cholesterol 25mg; Sodium 640mg; Total Carbohydrate 38g (Dietary Fiber 2g) **% Daily Value:** Vitamin A 25%; Vitamin C 25%; Calcium 30%; Iron 15% **Exchanges:** 2 Starch, ½ Other Carbohydrate, 1½ Lean Meat, 1½ Fat **Carbohydrate Choices:** 2½

This dinner recipe is easy, quick to make and healthy . . . and delicious, too!

Tomato and Cheese Pasta Skillet

 **Superfast**

Prep Time: 20 Minutes

Start to Finish:
20 Minutes

4 servings (1 cup each)

1 can (15 oz) Italian-style tomato sauce

1¾ cups water

1 package (7 oz) small pasta shells

2 tablespoons finely chopped onion

¾ cup shredded mozzarella cheese (3 oz)

1 In 8-inch skillet, mix tomato sauce, water, pasta and onion. Heat to boiling. Reduce heat to medium-low; cover and simmer 12 minutes, stirring occasionally.

2 Sprinkle cheese on top. Cover; cook 1 minute longer or until cheese is melted.

1 Serving: Calories 310 (Calories from Fat 50); Total Fat 6g (Saturated Fat 3g; Trans Fat 0g); Cholesterol 10mg; Sodium 670mg; Total Carbohydrate 49g (Dietary Fiber 4g) **% Daily Value:** Vitamin A 10%; Vitamin C 6%; Calcium 20%; Iron 15% **Exchanges:** 3 Starch, 1 Vegetable, ½ Medium-Fat Meat **Carbohydrate Choices:** 3

Beef with Mushrooms and Noodles

 **Superfast**

Prep Time: 20 Minutes
Start to Finish:
20 Minutes
4 servings (1¼ cups each)

3½ cups uncooked medium egg noodles (6 oz)

½ lb boneless beef sirloin steak, cut into thin bite-size strips

¼ teaspoon peppered seasoned salt

1 can (15 oz) Italian-style tomato sauce

1 package (8 oz) sliced fresh mushrooms (3 cups)

6 small green onions, cut into ½-inch pieces

1 Cook and drain noodles as directed on package, omitting salt. Place on serving platter or in serving bowl; cover to keep warm.

2 Meanwhile, sprinkle beef with peppered seasoned salt. Heat 10-inch nonstick skillet over medium-high heat. Add beef; cook and stir 2 minutes or until brown.

3 Stir in tomato sauce, mushrooms and onions (if necessary, break up larger pieces of tomatoes with spoon). Heat to boiling. Reduce heat to low; simmer uncovered 3 to 5 minutes, stirring occasionally, until vegetables are tender. Pour beef mixture over noodles; toss gently to mix.

1 Serving: Calories 280 (Calories from Fat 45); Total Fat 4.5g (Saturated Fat 1g; Trans Fat 0g); Cholesterol 70mg; Sodium 670mg; Total Carbohydrate 36g (Dietary Fiber 3g) **% Daily Value:** Vitamin A 10%; Vitamin C 8%; Calcium 4%; Iron 25% **Exchanges:** 2 Starch, ½ Other Carbohydrate, 2½ Very Lean Meat **Carbohydrate Choices:** 2½

Save even more time by using canned mushrooms instead of the presliced fresh ones.

Pork Chops Cubano with Garlic-Citrus Sauce

Prep Time: 15 Minutes
Start to Finish: 35 Minutes
4 servings

PORK CHOPS

1 cup Fiber One cereal

1 tablespoon finely chopped fresh cilantro

1 teaspoon finely chopped garlic

2 teaspoons grated orange peel

1 teaspoon onion powder

1 teaspoon dried oregano leaves

1 teaspoon ground cumin

¼ teaspoon pepper

4 pork loin chops, ½ inch thick (4 oz each)

¼ cup buttermilk

2 teaspoons olive or canola oil

GARLIC-CITRUS SAUCE

2 teaspoons olive or canola oil

1 tablespoon finely chopped garlic

¼ cup lime juice

2 tablespoons orange juice

2 tablespoons chopped fresh cilantro

1 Place cereal in resealable food-storage plastic bag; seal bag and crush with rolling pin or meat mallet (or crush in food processor).

2 In shallow dish, mix cereal, 1 tablespoon cilantro, 1 teaspoon garlic, the orange peel, onion powder, oregano, cumin and pepper. Dip pork chops into buttermilk; coat completely with cereal mixture.

3 In 10-inch nonstick skillet, heat 2 teaspoons oil. Add pork chops; cook over medium heat 9 minutes. Turn; cook 5 to 8 longer minutes or until pork is no longer pink in center.

4 Meanwhile, in 1-quart saucepan, heat 2 teaspoons oil over medium heat. Cook 1 tablespoon garlic in oil about 1 minute, stirring occasionally, until golden. Stir in lime and orange juices. Heat to boiling, stirring occasionally. Remove from heat; stir in 2 tablespoons cilantro. Cover; refrigerate until serving time. Serve with pork chops.

1 Serving: Calories 300 (Calories from Fat 120); Total Fat 14g (Saturated Fat 3.5g; Trans Fat 0g); Cholesterol 70mg; Sodium 115mg; Total Carbohydrate 17g (Dietary Fiber 7g) **% Daily Value:** Vitamin A 8%; Vitamin C 10%; Calcium 10%; Iron 20% **Exchanges:** 1 Starch, 3 Lean Meat, 1 Fat **Carbohydrate Choices:** 1

To get the most juice from the orange, microwave on High for a few seconds or roll it around on a countertop a few times while applying gentle pressure before squeezing it.

Honey Mustard–Glazed Pork Chops

 **Superfast**

Prep Time: 15 Minutes
Start to Finish:
15 Minutes

4 servings

⅓ **cup honey**

2 tablespoons yellow mustard

⅛ **teaspoon ground cloves**

½ **teaspoon onion salt**

¼ **teaspoon pepper**

**4 boneless pork loin chops,
¾ inch thick (1 lb)**

Orange slices, if desired

1 In small bowl, mix honey, mustard and cloves. Sprinkle onion salt and pepper over pork chops.

2 Heat 10-inch nonstick skillet over medium-high heat. Add pork chops; cook 3 minutes. Turn pork. Reduce heat to medium-low; pour honey mixture over pork chops. Cover; cook 5 to 8 minutes longer or until pork is no longer pink and meat thermometer inserted in center of pork reads 160°F. Garnish with orange slices.

1 Serving: Calories 270 (Calories from Fat 80); Total Fat 9g (Saturated Fat 3g; Trans Fat 0g); Cholesterol 70mg; Sodium 330mg; Total Carbohydrate 24g (Dietary Fiber 0g) **% Daily Value:** Vitamin A 0%; Vitamin C 0%; Calcium 0%; Iron 6% **Exchanges:** 1½ Other Carbohydrate, 3½ Lean Meat **Carbohydrate Choices:** 1½

Home-Style Sausage and Potato Skillet

Prep Time: 30 Minutes

Start to Finish:
30 Minutes

4 servings (1¼ cups each)

¾ lb bulk light turkey and pork sausage

1 large or 2 medium onions, chopped (1 cup)

2 lb red potatoes (about 12 medium), unpeeled, very thinly sliced

1 cup water

½ teaspoon salt

½ teaspoon paprika

¼ teaspoon dried thyme leaves

⅛ teaspoon pepper

1 Heat nonstick Dutch oven over medium-high heat. Add sausage; cook 4 to 5 minutes, stirring frequently, until no longer pink. Remove sausage from Dutch oven; drain on paper towels. Set aside.

2 Wipe Dutch oven clean with paper towels. Add onions; cook over medium heat about 5 minutes, stirring occasionally.

3 Gently stir in cooked sausage and remaining ingredients. Heat to boiling. Reduce heat to medium-low; cover tightly and cook 8 to 10 minutes, stirring occasionally, just until potatoes are tender.

4 Remove from heat; gently stir mixture. Let stand covered 10 minutes to allow flavors to blend and light sauce to form.

1 Serving: Calories 360 (Calories from Fat 80); Total Fat 9g (Saturated Fat 2g; Trans Fat 0g); Cholesterol 80mg; Sodium 880mg; Total Carbohydrate 44g (Dietary Fiber 6g) **% Daily Value:** Vitamin A 4%; Vitamin C 25%; Calcium 8%; Iron 30% **Exchanges:** 3 Starch, 2 Lean Meat **Carbohydrate Choices:** 3

Spicy Chinese Chicken Tacos

 **Superfast**

Prep Time: 20 Minutes

Start to Finish: 20 Minutes

6 servings (2 tacos each)

1 box (4.6 oz) taco shells (12 shells)

3 boneless skinless chicken breasts (¾ lb), cut into thin bite-size strips

1 teaspoon grated gingerroot

1 small clove garlic, finely chopped

2 tablespoons soy sauce

1 tablespoon honey

1 large green onion, sliced

½ teaspoon crushed red pepper flakes

1½ cups shredded iceberg lettuce

1 If desired, heat taco shells as directed on box.

2 Heat 10-inch nonstick skillet over medium-high heat. Add chicken, gingerroot and garlic; cook 3 to 5 minutes, stirring frequently, until lightly browned.

3 Stir in soy sauce, honey, onion and pepper flakes to coat. Reduce heat to low; cover and cook 5 minutes, stirring occasionally, until chicken is no longer pink in center.

4 To serve, place slightly less than ¼ cup chicken mixture in each taco shell. Top each with lettuce. Serve immediately.

1 Serving: Calories 190 (Calories from Fat 60); Total Fat 7g (Saturated Fat 1.5g; Trans Fat 1g); Cholesterol 35mg; Sodium 420mg; Total Carbohydrate 18g (Dietary Fiber 1g) **% Daily Value:** Vitamin A 4%; Vitamin C 0%; Calcium 4%; Iron 6% **Exchanges:** 1 Starch, 1½ Lean Meat, ½ Fat **Carbohydrate Choices:** 1

turn down the heat

While a glass of water might seem ideal to douse a peppery "fire" in the mouth, a mild starch such as bread or rice or a dairy product (milk or yogurt) works better to neutralize the heat from hot chiles.

Southwest Chicken Hash Browns

Prep Time: 30 Minutes
Start to Finish:
30 Minutes
2 servings

2 boneless skinless chicken breasts, cut into ¼- to ½-inch pieces

½ cup finely chopped red onion

1 large red potato, shredded (about 1¾ cups)

4 teaspoons chopped fresh cilantro, if desired

½ teaspoon salt

1 tablespoon olive or canola oil

¼ cup fat-free sour cream

¼ cup chunky-style salsa

1 In medium bowl, mix chicken and onion. Rinse shredded potatoes with cold water; drain on paper towels. Add to chicken mixture. Stir in cilantro and salt.

2 In 10-inch nonstick skillet, heat 2 teaspoons of the oil over medium-high heat. Spread potato mixture evenly in skillet. Cook, without stirring, 6 to 9 minutes or until chicken is no longer pink in center and bottom of potato mixture is golden brown and crisp.

3 Place large plate over skillet; turn potato mixture upside down onto plate. Add remaining teaspoon oil to skillet. Slip potato mixture back into skillet, browned side up; cook 5 to 7 minutes, pressing lightly with pancake turner, until golden brown and crisp.

4 With pancake turner, divide chicken mixture in half; place on 2 plates. Top each with sour cream and salsa.

1 Serving: Calories 380 (Calories from Fat 100); Total Fat 11g (Saturated Fat 2g; Trans Fat 0g); Cholesterol 75mg; Sodium 900mg; Total Carbohydrate 40g (Dietary Fiber 4g) **% Daily Value:** Vitamin A 4%; Vitamin C 10%; Calcium 8%; Iron 10% **Exchanges:** 1½ Starch, 1 Other Carbohydrate, 3½ Lean Meat **Carbohydrate Choices:** 2½

Turkey and Twists in Tomato-Cream Sauce

 **Superfast**

Prep Time: 20 Minutes

Start to Finish:
20 Minutes

4 servings (1¾ cups each)

3 cups uncooked rotini pasta (8 oz)

⅓ lb cooked honey-roasted turkey breast

1 container (15 oz) refrigerated marinara sauce

½ cup reduced-fat sour cream

2 tablespoons finely shredded Parmesan cheese

2 tablespoons chopped fresh parsley

1 In 3-quart saucepan, cook pasta as directed on package, omitting salt. Drain; cover to keep warm.

2 Meanwhile, cut turkey into 1×¼×¼-inch strips. In 8-inch skillet, heat marinara sauce over medium heat. Stir in sour cream until well blended. Stir in turkey; cook until hot.

3 Serve cooked sauce over pasta. Sprinkle with cheese and parsley.

1 Serving: Calories 450 (Calories from Fat 90); Total Fat 10g (Saturated Fat 4g; Trans Fat 0g); Cholesterol 40mg; Sodium 610mg; Total Carbohydrate 69g (Dietary Fiber 4g) **% Daily Value:** Vitamin A 15%; Vitamin C 10%; Calcium 10%; Iron 20% **Exchanges:** 2½ Starch, 2 Other Carbohydrate, 2 Lean Meat, ½ Fat **Carbohydrate Choices:** 4½

Terrific Turkey Burgers

Prep Time: 25 Minutes

Start to Finish:
25 Minutes

8 sandwiches

2 lb lean (at least 90%) ground turkey

1 cup unseasoned dry bread crumbs

⅔ cup finely chopped onion

½ cup ketchup or tomato sauce

2 tablespoons lemon juice

4 teaspoons soy sauce

4 teaspoons Worcestershire sauce

¼ teaspoon pepper

8 whole wheat burger buns, split

Lettuce, if desired

1 Heat gas or charcoal grill. In large bowl, mix all ingredients except buns and lettuce until well blended. Shape mixture into 8 patties, ½ inch thick.

2 Lightly oil grill rack. Place patties on grill over medium heat. Cover grill; cook 10 to 12 minutes, turning once, until meat thermometer inserted in center of patties reads 165°F.

3 Meanwhile, place buns cut sides down on grill. Cook 1 to 2 minutes or until lightly toasted. Place patties in lettuce-lined buns. If desired, serve with additional ketchup and pickle slices.

To Broil Patties: Place on sprayed broiler pan; broil 4 to 6 inches from heat using times in the recipe as a guide, turning once. Place buns, cut side up, on broiler pan; broil 1 to 2 minutes.

1 Sandwich: Calories 340 (Calories from Fat 80); Total Fat 9g (Saturated Fat 2g; Trans Fat 0g); Cholesterol 75mg; Sodium 720mg; Total Carbohydrate 34g (Dietary Fiber 4g) **% Daily Value:** Vitamin A 4%; Vitamin C 4%; Calcium 10%; Iron 15% **Exchanges:** 2 Starch, 3½ Lean Meat **Carbohydrate Choices:** 2

Wet your hands before shaping the ground turkey mixture into patties. The moisture on your hands makes it easier to shape the patties and eliminates sticking.

Tuna Salad Italiano

Prep Time: 30 Minutes

Start to Finish:
30 Minutes

8 servings (1 cup each)

2 cups uncooked small pasta shells (7 oz)

4 small red potatoes, cut in half, sliced

2 cups frozen cut green beans

1 tablespoon olive or canola oil

1 can (6 oz) tuna in water, drained, flaked

1 medium tomato, seeded, chopped (about ¾ cup)

8 medium green onions, sliced (½ cup)

½ cup Italian dressing

2 hard-cooked eggs, sliced

1 In 4-quart saucepan or Dutch oven, cook pasta as directed on package, adding potatoes and frozen green beans during last 5 to 7 minutes of cook time; cook until vegetables and pasta are tender. Drain.

2 In large bowl, gently toss cooked pasta, potatoes and green beans with oil.

3 Stir in tuna, tomato and onions. Pour dressing over salad; stir gently to coat. Top with hard-cooked eggs. Serve immediately or if you have more time, refrigerate salad until chilled.

1 Serving: Calories 290 (Calories from Fat 70); Total Fat 8g (Saturated Fat 1g; Trans Fat 0g); Cholesterol 60mg; Sodium 450mg; Total Carbohydrate 40g (Dietary Fiber 4g) **% Daily Value:** Vitamin A 8%; Vitamin C 25%; Calcium 4%; Iron 15% **Exchanges:** 2 Starch, ½ Other Carbohydrate, 1 Lean Meat, 1 Fat **Carbohydrate Choices:** 2½

Fresh green beans can be used in place of the frozen beans.

You could use salmon instead of the tuna in this easy pasta salad.

Lemon Butter Catfish Fillets

 **Superfast**

Prep Time: 20 Minutes
Start to Finish: 20 Minutes
4 servings

1 lb catfish fillets

1 cup water

2 teaspoons cornstarch

½ teaspoon chicken bouillon granules

Dash pepper

2 tablespoons all-natural butter-flavor granules

1 teaspoon grated lemon peel

1 tablespoon chopped fresh chives

1 Set oven control to broil. Line 15×10×1-inch pan with foil; spray foil with cooking spray. Pat catfish fillets dry with paper towels; place in pan.

2 Broil with tops 4 to 6 inches from heat 8 to 10 minutes, turning once, until fish flakes easily with fork.

3 Meanwhile, in 1-quart saucepan, mix water, cornstarch, bouillon and pepper until smooth. Cook over medium heat, stirring frequently, until bubbly and thickened. Reduce heat to low; stir in butter-flavor granules and lemon peel. Remove from heat; stir in chives. Serve sauce over fish.

1 Serving: Calories 170 (Calories from Fat 70); Total Fat 7g (Saturated Fat 1.5g; Trans Fat 0g); Cholesterol 85mg; Sodium 200mg; Total Carbohydrate 4g (Dietary Fiber 0g) **% Daily Value:** Vitamin A 0%; Vitamin C 2%; Calcium 6%; Iron 10% **Exchanges:** 3 Lean Meat **Carbohydrate Choices:** 0

Cheesy Potato and Sausage Frittata

Prep Time: 30 Minutes

Start to Finish:
30 Minutes

4 servings

6 oz bulk light turkey and pork sausage

4 cups frozen potatoes O'Brien with onions and peppers (from 28-oz bag)

1 carton (8 oz) fat-free egg product (1 cup) or 4 eggs, lightly beaten

¼ cup fat-free (skim) milk

⅛ teaspoon ground red pepper (cayenne)

⅛ teaspoon pepper

⅛ teaspoon fennel seed, crushed, if desired

½ cup finely shredded reduced-fat Cheddar cheese (2 oz)

1 Heat 12-inch nonstick skillet over high heat. Add sausage; cook 4 to 5 minutes, stirring frequently, until no longer pink. Remove sausage from skillet; drain on paper towels. Return sausage to skillet. Gently stir in potatoes.

2 In small bowl, mix egg product and remaining ingredients except cheese until well blended. Pour egg mixture evenly over potato mixture; cover and cook over medium-low heat 10 minutes.

3 Uncover; cook 5 to 8 minutes longer or until egg product mixture is set but still moist on top. Remove from heat. Sprinkle cheese over top. Let stand 3 to 5 minutes or until cheese is melted. Cut into wedges to serve.

1 Serving: Calories 220 (Calories from Fat 50); Total Fat 6g (Saturated Fat 1.5g; Trans Fat 0g); Cholesterol 40mg; Sodium 560mg; Total Carbohydrate 21g (Dietary Fiber 2g) **% Daily Value:** Vitamin A 15%; Vitamin C 6%; Calcium 15%; Iron 10% **Exchanges:** 1½ Starch, 2 Lean Meat **Carbohydrate Choices:** 1½

Italian Dinner Frittata

Prep Time: 15 Minutes

Start to Finish: 30 Minutes

4 servings

1 tablespoon canola oil

8 medium green onions, sliced (½ cup)

1 carton (16 oz) fat-free egg product or 8 eggs, beaten

½ cup shredded mozzarella cheese (2 oz)

½ cup chopped seeded tomato (1 small)

2 tablespoons chopped fresh parsley

⅛ teaspoon pepper

⅓ cup shredded Parmesan cheese

Additional chopped tomato, if desired

Additional chopped fresh parsley, if desired

1 In 10-inch nonstick skillet, heat oil over medium heat until hot. Cook onions in oil 2 to 3 minutes, stirring frequently, until tender.

2 Stir in egg product, mozzarella cheese, tomato, parsley and pepper. Reduce heat to medium-low; cover and cook 9 to 11 minutes or until egg product is set around edge and light brown on bottom.

3 Sprinkle Parmesan cheese on top. Cover; remove from heat and let stand 3 to 4 minutes or until cheese is melted. Garnish with additional chopped tomato and parsley.

1 Serving: Calories 180 (Calories from Fat 80); Total Fat 9g (Saturated Fat 3.5g; Trans Fat 0g); Cholesterol 15mg; Sodium 440mg; Total Carbohydrate 4g (Dietary Fiber 1g) **% Daily Value:** Vitamin A 40%; Vitamin C 6%; Calcium 25%; Iron 15% **Exchanges:** ½ Other Carbohydrate, 2½ Lean Meat **Carbohydrate Choices:** 0

what's egg substitute?

Egg substitute is a pasteurized egg white plus traces of vegetable gums (less than 1%) and coloring. It comes frozen or refrigerated in boxes that resemble milk cartons. Simply pour the amount needed: ¼ cup egg substitute = 1 whole fresh egg.

	1 LARGE EGG	1/4 CUP EGG SUBSTITUTE*
Calories	80	30
Protein	6 g	6 g
Carbohydrate	1 g	1 g
Fat	6 g	0 g
Cholesterol	270 mg	0 mg
Sodium	70 mg	100 mg

*Source: Egg Beaters package label

French Toast with Raspberry-Cranberry Syrup

Prep Time: 10 Minutes
Start to Finish:
30 Minutes
4 servings (2 slices each)

FRENCH TOAST

2 whole eggs plus 1 egg white, lightly beaten, or ½ cup fat-free egg product

1 cup fat-free (skim) milk

2 teaspoons rum extract

¼ teaspoon ground nutmeg

8 slices (1 inch thick) French bread

SYRUP

½ cup frozen (thawed) raspberry blend juice concentrate

½ cup jellied cranberry sauce

1 tablespoon powdered sugar

1 Heat oven to 425°F. In medium bowl, mix beaten eggs and egg white, the milk, rum extract and nutmeg until well blended.

2 Dip bread slices into egg mixture, coating both sides well. In ungreased 11×7-inch (2-quart) glass baking dish, place bread slices. Pour remaining egg mixture over bread slices. Let stand at room temperature 10 minutes.

3 Spray cookie sheet with cooking spray. Remove bread slices from dish; place on cookie sheet. Bake 12 to 15 minutes or until golden brown, turning slices once halfway through baking.

4 Meanwhile, in 1-quart saucepan, mix syrup ingredients; cook over medium-low heat, stirring occasionally, until cranberry sauce and sugar have melted. Serve French toast with syrup.

1 Serving: Calories 300 (Calories from Fat 40); Total Fat 4.5g (Saturated Fat 1.5g; Trans Fat 0g); Cholesterol 105mg; Sodium 340mg; Total Carbohydrate 55g (Dietary Fiber 2g) **% Daily Value:** Vitamin A 6%; Vitamin C 6%; Calcium 15%; Iron 10% **Exchanges:** 1½ Starch, 2 Other Carbohydrate, 1 Medium-Fat Meat **Carbohydrate Choices:** 3 ½

Crunchy French Toast

Prep Time: 30 Minutes

Start to Finish:
30 Minutes

5 servings (2 slices each)

2½ cups Whole Grain Total® cereal

2 eggs or ½ cup fat-free egg product

¾ cup orange juice

¼ teaspoon salt

10 slices (1 inch thick) whole-grain or regular French bread

1 Place cereal in resealable food-storage plastic bag; seal bag and crush with rolling pin or meat mallet. In shallow bowl, place crushed cereal; set aside. In medium bowl, beat eggs, orange juice and salt with wire whisk until well blended.

2 Spray griddle or 12-inch skillet with cooking spray; heat to 350°F or over medium heat. Dip each slice of bread into egg mixture, turning to coat both sides; coat with cereal. Place on griddle; cook 4 to 6 minutes, turning once, until golden brown on both sides.

Oven French Toast: Heat oven to 450°F. Generously grease bottom and sides of 15×10×1-inch pan with shortening. Prepare and dip as directed—except place bread in pan. Bake 5 to 8 minutes or until golden brown. Turn bread; bake 3 to 5 minutes longer or until golden brown.

1 Serving: Calories 410 (Calories from Fat 70); Total Fat 7g (Saturated Fat 1.5g; Trans Fat 1g); Cholesterol 85mg; Sodium 870mg; Total Carbohydrate 72g (Dietary Fiber 9g) **% Daily Value:** Vitamin A 10%; Vitamin C 45%; Calcium 80%; Iron 90% **Exchanges:** 3 Starch, 2 Other Carbohydrate, ½ Medium-Fat Meat, ½ Fat **Carbohydrate Choices:** 5

If you have a hard time finding whole-grain French bread ask your local grocer to carry it.

salads and sandwiches

chapter

5

Onion-Smothered Barbecued Turkey Burgers, see page 152

Spinach, Strawberry and Grapefruit Toss

Prep Time: 25 Minutes

Start to Finish: 25 Minutes

12 servings

ALMONDS AND DRESSING

3 tablespoons canola oil

⅓ cup sliced almonds

3 tablespoons honey

Dash ground cinnamon

½ teaspoon grated lime peel

3 tablespoons fresh lime juice

1 teaspoon Dijon mustard

¼ teaspoon salt

SALAD

1 bag (10 oz) washed fresh spinach leaves, torn (10 cups)

1 pint (2 cups) fresh strawberries, sliced

1 grapefruit, peeled, sectioned

1 Line cookie sheet with foil. Spray foil with cooking spray. In 6-inch skillet, heat 2 teaspoons of the oil over medium heat until hot. Add almonds; cook and stir until lightly browned. Add 1 tablespoon of the honey and the cinnamon; cook and stir 1 to 2 minutes longer or until almonds are glazed and golden brown. Place on foil-lined cookie sheet. Set aside to cool.

2 In jar with tight-fitting lid, shake remaining oil and remaining honey, the lime peel, lime juice, mustard and salt until well blended.

3 In large serving bowl, mix spinach, strawberries and grapefruit.

4 Just before serving, drizzle dressing over salad; toss lightly to coat. Sprinkle with toasted almonds.

1 Serving: Calories 90 (Calories from Fat 45); Total Fat 5g (Saturated Fat 0g; Trans Fat 0g); Cholesterol 0mg; Sodium 80mg; Total Carbohydrate 10g (Dietary Fiber 1g) **% Daily Value:** Vitamin A 45%; Vitamin C 50%; Calcium 4%; Iron 6% **Exchanges:** ½ Other Carbohydrate, 1 Fat **Carbohydrate Choices:** ½

To section a grapefruit, use a sharp serrated knife to remove its peel and outer membrane. Then, cut along one side of each section next to the dividing membrane, using the knife to help release the fruit from the membrane on the other side of the section. This method of sectioning citrus fruit is called "supreming" the fruit.

Honey-Lime Berries and Greens

 **Superfast**

Prep Time: 10 Minutes

Start to Finish:
10 Minutes

6 servings (1 cup each)

SALAD

6 cups mixed salad greens

¾ cup fresh raspberries or strawberries

4 thin red onion slices, separated into rings

2 tablespoons sliced almonds, if desired

DRESSING

¼ cup lime juice

3 tablespoons canola oil

3 tablespoons honey

¼ teaspoon poppy seed

¼ teaspoon Dijon mustard

1 In medium bowl, gently toss salad ingredients.

2 In jar with tight-fitting lid, shake dressing ingredients well.

3 Serve dressing with salad.

1 Servings: Calories 120 (Calories from Fat 60); Total Fat 7g (Saturated Fat 0.5g; Trans Fat 0g); Cholesterol 0mg; Sodium 25mg; Total Carbohydrate 13g (Dietary Fiber 1g) **% Daily Value:** Vitamin A 60%; Vitamin C 40%; Calcium 4%; Iron 4% **Exchanges:** 1 Other Carbohydrate, 1½ Fat **Carbohydrate Choices:** 1

purchasing prepared greens

Many greens are now available washed, torn and ready to dress, either in grocery store salad bars or in an increasing number of prepackaged options including romaine, coleslaw mix, mesclun (mixed young salad greens) and spinach. When purchasing packaged greens, look for bright color and crisp leaves with no signs of browning or wilting.

Use your favorite variety of Dijon mustard to make the dressing.

This salad can be made ahead, but hold off on dressing it until you're ready to serve.

Apple-Cranberry Salad

 **Superfast**

Prep Time: 15 Minutes

Start to Finish:
15 Minutes

6 servings (1 cup each)

5 cups torn romaine lettuce

1 medium unpeeled apple,
diced (1 cup)

½ cup sweetened dried
cranberries

¼ cup chopped green onions
(4 medium)

⅓ cup refrigerated poppy
seed dressing

1 In large serving bowl, place lettuce, apple, cranberries and onions.

2 Pour dressing over salad; toss to coat.

1 Serving: Calories 120 (Calories from Fat 50); Total Fat 6g (Saturated Fat 0.5g; Trans Fat 0g); Cholesterol 0mg; Sodium 95mg; Total Carbohydrate 16g (Dietary Fiber 2g) **% Daily Value:** Vitamin A 45%; Vitamin C 20%; Calcium 0%; Iron 2% **Exchanges:** 1 Other Carbohydrate, 1½ Fat **Carbohydrate Choices:** 1

- Try a ripe, red or yellow-green pear instead of the apple.

- Look for refrigerated poppy seed dressing in the produce section of your grocery store.

Tropical Romaine Salad

Prep Time: 30 Minutes

Start to Finish:
30 Minutes

6 servings (1¼ cups each)

DRESSING

1 teaspoon grated lime peel

3 tablespoons honey

2 tablespoons fresh lime juice

1 tablespoon olive oil

SALAD

2 cups frozen sugar snap peas (from 1-lb bag)

4 cups torn romaine lettuce

1 avocado, peeled, pitted and cut into ½-inch cubes

1 large ripe mango, peeled, seed removed and cut into ½-inch cubes

¼ cup red onion strips

¼ cup shredded coconut

1 In small bowl, mix dressing ingredients.

2 Cook sugar snap peas as directed on bag; drain. Rinse with cold water to cool; drain well.

3 In large bowl, mix cooked peas, lettuce, avocado, mango and onion. Add dressing; toss to coat. Sprinkle with coconut.

1 Serving: Calories 170 (Calories from Fat 70); Total Fat 7g (Saturated Fat 2g; Trans Fat 0g); Cholesterol 0mg; Sodium 20mg; Total Carbohydrate 24g (Dietary Fiber 4g) **% Daily Value:** Vitamin A 50%; Vitamin C 50%; Calcium 4%; Iron 10% **Exchanges:** ½ Fruit, ½ Other Carbohydrate, 1 Vegetable, 1½ Fat **Carbohydrate Choices:** 1½

accent on avocados

Look for unblemished avocados that are heavy for their size. To judge ripeness, press the avocado between your palms; if it yields to pressure, it's ripe. If it's not ripe, let it stand at room temperature for a few days. Or speed up the ripening process by placing the avocado in a paper bag and let it stand on the counter; check it daily for ripeness. Refrigerate ripe avocados if you won't use them right away.

Two varieties of avocados most common in the U.S.:

- Hass avocado, grown mostly in California and available year-round, is oval shaped with pebbly textured green skin that turns black when ripe.

- Fuerte avocado is pear-shaped, larger and has thin, smooth skin that remains green as it ripens.

Layered Piña Colada Chicken Salad

 **Superfast**

Prep Time: 15 Minutes
Start to Finish:
15 Minutes
6 servings (1½ cups each)

DRESSING

1 container (6 oz) piña colada low-fat yogurt

1½ to 2 tablespoons fresh lime juice

1 teaspoon Caribbean jerk seasoning (dry)

SALAD

3 cups shredded romaine lettuce

2 cups cubed cooked chicken

1 can (15 oz) black beans, drained, rinsed

1½ cups diced peeled ripe mango

1 cup chopped seeded plum (Roma) tomatoes (2 to 3 medium)

½ cup shredded reduced-fat Cheddar cheese (2 oz)

½ cup thinly sliced green onions (8 medium)

½ cup slivered almonds

1 In small bowl, mix dressing ingredients until well blended.

2 In 3- or 4-quart clear glass serving bowl, layer salad ingredients except almonds in order listed. Spoon dressing evenly over salad; sprinkle with almonds.

1 Serving: Calories 330 (Calories from Fat 90); Total Fat 10g (Saturated Fat 2.5g; Trans Fat 0g); Cholesterol 45mg; Sodium 290mg; Total Carbohydrate 32g (Dietary Fiber 9g) **% Daily Value:** Vitamin A 40%; Vitamin C 40%; Calcium 30%; Iron 15% **Exchanges:** 1 Starch, 1 Other Carbohydrate, 3½ Lean Meat **Carbohydrate Choices:** 2

Layered Salad Supreme

 **Superfast**

Prep Time: 15 Minutes

Start to Finish:
15 Minutes

12 servings

SALAD

5 cups torn lettuce

2½ cups broccoli florets

2 cups julienne (matchstick-cut) carrots

1 can (15 oz) chick peas or garbanzo beans, drained, rinsed

1 small red onion, thinly sliced

DRESSING

¾ cup fat-free mayonnaise or salad dressing

⅓ cup fat-free (skim) milk

½ cup grated Parmesan cheese

2 tablespoons chopped fresh parsley

1 In 3-quart glass bowl with straight sides, layer lettuce, broccoli, carrots, beans and onion slices.

2 In small bowl, mix mayonnaise, milk and Parmesan cheese until well blended. Spread dressing evenly over salad. Sprinkle with parsley. Serve immediately, or cover and refrigerate until serving.

1 Serving: Calories 110 (Calories from Fat 25); Total Fat 2.5g (Saturated Fat 1g; Trans Fat 0g); Cholesterol 5mg; Sodium 210mg; Total Carbohydrate 15g (Dietary Fiber 3g) **% Daily Value:** Vitamin A 80%; Vitamin C 35%; Calcium 10%; Iron 8% **Exchanges:** ½ Other Carbohydrate, 1 Vegetable, ½ Lean Meat, ½ Fat **Carbohydrate Choices:** 1

If you don't have the large glass bowl, the salad can be layered in a 13×9-inch (three-quart) glass baking dish instead.

Chicken and Mango Salad in Lettuce Bowls

 **Superfast**

Prep Time: 15 Minutes

Start to Finish:
20 Minutes

6 servings (1¼ cups each)

1 cup frozen shoepeg white corn

1½ cups chopped deli rotisserie chicken (without skin)

¾ cup shredded Colby-Monterey Jack cheese blend (3 oz)

½ cup chopped red bell pepper

½ cup fat-free ranch dressing

1 small cucumber, cut in half lengthwise, cut into ¼-inch slices

1 jar (1 lb 8 oz) refrigerated mango, cut into chunks, or 1½ cups chopped peeled fresh mango (about 2)

1 can (15 oz) black beans, drained, rinsed

1 large head Boston or Bibb lettuce, center removed

1 Cook corn as directed on bag until crisp-tender. Drain; rinse with cold water to cool.

2 In large bowl, place corn and remaining ingredients except lettuce; toss gently to mix.

3 Place lettuce on serving plate; spoon chicken mixture into lettuce.

1 Serving: Calories 360 (Calories from Fat 90); Total Fat 10g (Saturated Fat 4.5g; Trans Fat 0g); Cholesterol 50mg; Sodium 450mg; Total Carbohydrate 47g (Dietary Fiber 8g) **% Daily Value:** Vitamin A 45%; Vitamin C 120%; Calcium 20%; Iron 15% **Exchanges:** 2 Starch, 1 Fruit, 2 Lean Meat, ½ Fat **Carbohydrate Choices:** 3

Avocado would make a nice addition to this recipe. Just chop half of a medium avocado and stir into the chicken mixture. Slice the remaining half of avocado to use as a garnish.

Chicken, Spring Vegetable and Pasta Salad

Prep Time: 25 Minutes

Start to Finish:
25 Minutes

4 servings (1½ cups each)

SALAD

8 oz fresh asparagus spears

2 cups uncooked penne or mostaccioli pasta (6 to 7 oz)

1⅓ cups ready-to-eat baby-cut carrots (about 6 oz), quartered lengthwise

½ cup frozen baby sweet peas

2 cups cubed cooked chicken

DRESSING

1 container (6 oz) lemon burst low-fat yogurt

¼ cup fat-free mayonnaise or salad dressing

2 tablespoons chopped fresh chives

¼ teaspoon salt

⅛ teaspoon pepper

1 clove garlic, finely chopped

1 Break off tough ends of asparagus spears; cut asparagus into 1-inch pieces. Cook pasta as directed on package, adding asparagus, carrots and peas during last 5 to 7 minutes of cook time; cook until asparagus is crisp-tender. Drain; rinse with cold water to cool. Drain well.

2 In large bowl, mix cooked pasta mixture and chicken.

3 In small bowl, mix dressing ingredients until well blended. Pour over salad; toss gently to coat. Serve immediately, or cover and refrigerate until serving time. If desired, garnish with additional chives.

1 Serving: Calories 400 (Calories from Fat 70); Total Fat 7g (Saturated Fat 2g; Trans Fat 0g); Cholesterol 65mg; Sodium 550mg; Total Carbohydrate 52g (Dietary Fiber 5g) **% Daily Value:** Vitamin A 150%; Vitamin C 6%; Calcium 10%; Iron 20% **Exchanges:** 2 Starch, 1 Other Carbohydrate, 1 Vegetable, 3 Lean Meat **Carbohydrate Choices:** 3½

Turkey can be substituted for the chicken. If you want more flavor, use smoked turkey.

This recipe also tastes great with shrimp instead of chicken.

Asian Coleslaw Salad

 **Superfast**

Prep Time: 10 Minutes

Start to Finish:
10 Minutes

14 servings (½ cup each)

1 box (9 oz) frozen sugar snap
peas

1 bag (16 oz) coleslaw mix
(shredded cabbage and
carrots)

1 cup thin bite-size red bell
pepper strips

1 cup shredded carrots
(1½ medium)

1 package (3 oz) Oriental-
flavor ramen noodle soup mix

1 cup sweet-and-sour sauce

2 tablespoons soy sauce

1 Cook and drain peas as directed on box. Cool 1 minute.

2 Meanwhile, in large serving bowl, toss coleslaw mix, bell
pepper and carrots. Discard seasoning packet from soup mix;
break noodles into bite-size pieces, and add to salad. Add
peas to salad.

3 In small bowl, mix sweet-and-sour sauce and soy sauce; pour
over salad, and toss gently.

1 Serving: Calories 50 (Calories from Fat 5); Total Fat 1g (Saturated Fat 0g; Trans Fat 0g);
Cholesterol 0mg; Sodium 230mg; Total Carbohydrate 10g (Dietary Fiber 2g) **% Daily Value:**
Vitamin A 60%; Vitamin C 35%; Calcium 2%; Iron 4% **Exchanges:** ½ Other Carbohydrate,
1 Vegetable **Carbohydrate Choices:** ½

- If the sweet-and-sour sauce that you are using is not
  sweet enough for your taste, go ahead and add one to
  two teaspoons honey to the dressing mixture.

- Ramen noodles give this salad crunch but if you
  prefer, cover the salad for an hour for softer noodles.

Asian Noodle Salad

 **Superfast**

Prep Time: 20 Minutes
Start to Finish:
20 Minutes
12 servings (1 cup each)

SALAD

1 bag (10 oz) Italian-style mixed salad greens

2 cups julienne (matchstick-cut) carrots (from 10-oz bag)

2 cans (8 oz each) sliced water chestnuts, drained

1 can (11 oz) mandarin orange segments, drained

⅓ cup sliced green onions (5 to 6 medium)

1 tablespoon sesame seed, toasted if desired*

½ cup chow mein noodles

DRESSING

2 tablespoons sugar

½ teaspoon ground ginger

¼ teaspoon salt

3 tablespoons vinegar

1 teaspoon red pepper sauce

1 teaspoon soy sauce

2 tablespoons canola oil

1 In 13×9-inch (3-quart) glass baking dish, layer salad greens, carrots, water chestnuts, orange segments and onions. Sprinkle with sesame seed.

2 In small bowl, mix all dressing ingredients except oil with wire whisk. Gradually add oil, beating until well blended. Drizzle dressing evenly over salad. Top with chow mein noodles.

*To toast sesame seed, sprinkle in ungreased heavy skillet. Cook over medium-low heat 5 to 7 minutes, stirring frequently until browning begins, then stirring constantly until golden brown.

1 Serving: Calories 90 (Calories from Fat 30); Total Fat 3.5g (Saturated Fat 0g; Trans Fat 0g); Cholesterol 0mg; Sodium 110mg; Total Carbohydrate 13g (Dietary Fiber 2g) **% Daily Value:** Vitamin A 100%; Vitamin C 25%; Calcium 2%; Iron 4% **Exchanges:** 1 Other Carbohydrate, ½ Fat **Carbohydrate Choices:** 1

- For a bit of extra sesame flavor, use one teaspoon sesame oil instead of the soy sauce in the dressing.

- Look for wide chow mein noodles for a fun garnish for the salad.

Barley, Corn and Pepper Salad

Prep Time: 30 Minutes
Start to Finish:
30 Minutes
10 servings (½ cup each)

SALAD

1 cup uncooked quick-cooking barley

1¼ cups frozen whole kernel corn

½ cup red bell pepper strips

½ cup chopped green bell pepper

½ cup sliced green onions (8 medium)

DRESSING

¼ cup olive oil

¼ cup lemon juice

¼ cup chopped fresh cilantro

½ teaspoon salt

Coarse ground black pepper

1 Cook barley to desired doneness as directed on package. Drain; rinse with cold water. Cook corn as directed on bag. Drain; rinse with cold water.

2 In large bowl, mix barley, corn and remaining salad ingredients.

3 In jar with tight-fitting lid, shake dressing ingredients well. Pour dressing over salad; toss gently to coat. Serve at room temperature or chilled. Cover and refrigerate any remaining salad.

1 Serving: Calories 150 (Calories from Fat 50); Total Fat 6g (Saturated Fat 1g; Trans Fat 0g); Cholesterol 0mg; Sodium 125mg; Total Carbohydrate 21g (Dietary Fiber 4g) **% Daily Value:** Vitamin A 6%; Vitamin C 25%; Calcium 0%; Iron 4% **Exchanges:** 1 Starch, ½ Other Carbohydrate, 1 Fat **Carbohydrate Choices:** 1½

Barley contains protein, fiber, B vitamins and several minerals. Quick-cooking barley doesn't require presoaking and, as its name implies, is quick to cook.

Warm Honey-Mustard Potato Salad

 **Superfast**

Prep Time: 10 Minutes

Start to Finish:
15 Minutes

12 servings (½ cup each)

1 bag (20 oz) refrigerated red potato wedges with skins (4 cups)

¼ cup honey

¼ cup yellow mustard

1 cup sliced celery (2 medium stalks)

½ cup chopped red bell pepper

2 tablespoons chopped green onions (2 medium) or red onion

¼ teaspoon garlic powder

¼ teaspoon salt

⅛ teaspoon coarse ground black pepper

1 In 2-quart microwavable casserole, place potatoes; cover. Microwave on High 3 to 5 minutes or until desired doneness. Cool slightly, about 5 minutes.

2 Meanwhile, in small bowl, mix honey and mustard until well blended.

3 Add remaining ingredients to potatoes in casserole. Pour honey mixture over salad; mix gently to coat.

1 Serving: Calories 60 (Calories from Fat 0); Total Fat 0g (Saturated Fat 0g; Trans Fat 0g); Cholesterol 0mg; Sodium 170mg; Total Carbohydrate 13g (Dietary Fiber 1g) **% Daily Value:** Vitamin A 4%; Vitamin C 15%; Calcium 0%; Iron 2% **Exchanges:** ½ Starch, ½ Other Carbohydrate **Carbohydrate Choices:** 1

You can use frozen potato wedges to make the salad. Microwave them as directed for five to eight minutes.

Mixed Fruit and Cheese Salad

 **Superfast**

Prep Time: 15 Minutes

Start to Finish: 15 Minutes

6 servings (½ cup each)

¾ **cup sliced fresh strawberries**

1 tablespoon poppy seed dressing

¾ **teaspoon sugar**

1 cup 1-inch pieces cantaloupe

½ **cup grapes, cut in half**

½ **cup fresh blueberries**

1 oz white Cheddar cheese, cut into ½-inch cubes

1 In food processor, place ¼ cup of the strawberries, the dressing and sugar. Cover; process, using quick on-and-off motions, until smooth.

2 In medium bowl, mix remaining ½ cup strawberries, the cantaloupe, grapes, blueberries and cheese. Pour dressing over fruit mixture; toss.

1 Serving: Calories 70 (Calories from Fat 25); Total Fat 2.5g (Saturated Fat 1g; Trans Fat 0g); Cholesterol 5mg; Sodium 50mg; Total Carbohydrate 9g (Dietary Fiber 1g) **% Daily Value:** Vitamin A 20%; Vitamin C 40%; Calcium 4%; Iron 0% **Exchanges:** ½ Fruit, ½ Other Carbohydrate, ½ Fat **Carbohydrate Choices:** ½

- Shave prep time by purchasing precut cantaloupe.

- Adding cheese to your salad is an easy way to include more calcium in your diet.

Gingered Fresh Fruit Salad

Prep Time: 25 Minutes

Start to Finish:
25 Minutes

8 servings (¾ cup each)

DRESSING

2 tablespoons honey

1 teaspoon chopped crystallized ginger

¼ teaspoon grated lime peel

2 tablespoons fresh lime juice

SALAD

2 cups fresh pineapple cubes

1 cup watermelon cubes

1 cup cantaloupe cubes

1 cup seedless green grapes

1 pint (2 cups) fresh raspberries

1 In 1-cup microwavable measuring cup, mix dressing ingredients. Microwave uncovered on High 20 to 30 seconds or until hot. Cool completely, about 15 minutes.

2 In very large bowl, mix salad ingredients. Pour dressing over fruit; toss gently to coat.

1 Serving: Calories 90 (Calories from Fat 0); Total Fat 0g (Saturated Fat 0g; Trans Fat 0g); Cholesterol 0mg; Sodium 5mg; Total Carbohydrate 20g (Dietary Fiber 3g) **% Daily Value:** Vitamin A 15%; Vitamin C 60%; Calcium 0%; Iron 2% **Exchanges:** 1 Fruit, ½ Other Carbohydrate **Carbohydrate Choices:** 1

Shorten prep time by purchasing precut watermelon and cantaloupe.

Serve this salad in a hollowed-out watermelon shell. If necessary, trim a thin piece from the bottom of the melon so the shell sits flat.

Fresh Fruit Salad with Poppy Seed Dressing

 **Superfast**

Prep Time: 15 Minutes

Start to Finish:
15 Minutes

8 servings

DRESSING

½ **cup honey**

¼ **cup frozen limeade concentrate, thawed**

¼ **cup canola oil**

1 **teaspoon grated orange peel**

½ **teaspoon poppy seed**

¼ **teaspoon ground mustard**

SALAD

2 **cups fresh blueberries**

4 **medium peaches, peeled, sliced**

4 **medium oranges, peeled, sliced**

4 **kiwifruit, peeled, sliced**

1 In small bowl, mix dressing ingredients with wire whisk until well blended.

2 Arrange salad ingredients in individual salad bowls. Serve with dressing.

1 Serving: Calories 270 (Calories from Fat 70); Total Fat 8g (Saturated Fat 0.5g; Trans Fat 0g); Cholesterol 0mg; Sodium 0mg; Total Carbohydrate 49g (Dietary Fiber 5g) **% Daily Value:** Vitamin A 8%; Vitamin C 130%; Calcium 6%; Iron 4% **Exchanges:** 2 Fruit, 1 Other Carbohydrate, 2 Fat **Carbohydrate Choices:** 3

If fresh peaches are not available, use frozen peaches and thaw them.

Pudding Fruit Salad

 **Superfast**

Prep Time: 20 Minutes

Start to Finish:
20 Minutes

9 servings (½ cup each)

1 container (4 oz) refrigerated vanilla pudding

½ cup frozen (thawed) whipped topping

1 cup seedless green grapes, halved

1 cup miniature marshmallows

1 can (11 oz) mandarin orange segments, drained

1 can (8 oz) pineapple tidbits in juice, drained

1 cup fresh strawberries, sliced

1 In medium bowl, mix pudding and whipped topping.

2 Gently stir in grapes, marshmallows, oranges and pineapple. Add strawberries; toss gently to coat. Serve immediately, or cover and refrigerate up to 8 hours before serving.

1 Serving: Calories 90 (Calories from Fat 10); Total Fat 1.5g (Saturated Fat 1g; Trans Fat 0g); Cholesterol 0mg; Sodium 25mg; Total Carbohydrate 18g (Dietary Fiber 1g) **% Daily Value:** Vitamin A 8%; Vitamin C 40%; Calcium 2%; Iron 0% **Exchanges:** ½ Fruit, ½ Other Carbohydrate, ½ Fat **Carbohydrate Choices:** 1

picking pineapple

To choose a pineapple, close your eyes and smell. The sweetest pineapples have the sweetest aroma, and that's the single best predictor of flavor. A pineapple's sweetness doesn't continue to develop after the fruit is picked.

Choose large, plump pineapple with bright color, fresh green leaves and no soft spots, decay on the bottom or fermented odor. Pineapples are available year-round, but the best prices generally can be found between April and June.

Tropical Fruit Salad with Yogurt-Apricot Dressing

 **Superfast**

Prep Time: 20 Minutes

Start to Finish:
20 Minutes

6 servings

DRESSING

½ **cup plain yogurt**

2 **tablespoons apricot preserves or orange marmalade**

¼ **teaspoon poppy seed**

SALAD

1 **small pineapple, peeled, cored and cut into wedges***

1 **medium mango or papaya, peeled, seeded and sliced (about 1½ cups)**

1 **medium banana, sliced (about 1 cup)**

2 **kiwifruit, peeled, sliced (about ⅔ cup)**

½ **cup seedless red grapes**

2 **tablespoons coconut, toasted if desired****

1   In small bowl, mix dressing ingredients.

2   On serving platter, arrange fruit in decorative pattern; sprinkle with coconut. Drizzle dressing over salad.

*To cut fresh pineapple, with long sharp knife, cut ½-inch slice off top and bottom of pineapple. Cut pineapple lengthwise into quarters. Cut fruit from rind; cut off core. Cut fruit into wedges.

**To toast coconut, heat oven to 350°F. Spread in ungreased shallow pan. Bake uncovered 6 to 10 minutes, stirring occasionally, until golden brown.

1 Serving: Calories 140 (Calories from Fat 5); Total Fat 0.5g (Saturated Fat 0g; Trans Fat 0g); Cholesterol 0mg; Sodium 15mg; Total Carbohydrate 32g (Dietary Fiber 3g) **% Daily Value:** Vitamin A 8%; Vitamin C 100%; Calcium 6%; Iron 2% **Exchanges:** 1 Fruit, 1 Other Carbohydrate **Carbohydrate Choices:** 2

You could easily substitute three-quarter cup refrigerated poppy seed dressing for the dressing mixture in this recipe.

Chicken and Apple "Clams"

 **Superfast**

Prep Time: 15 Minutes

Start to Finish:
15 Minutes

6 sandwiches

3 tablespoons mayonnaise or salad dressing

3 tablespoons plain fat-free yogurt

⅛ teaspoon seasoned salt

1 cup chopped cooked chicken breast

1 medium tart-sweet red apple, cored, cut into bite-size pieces (about ¾ cup)

3 tablespoons thinly sliced celery

6 whole wheat or white mini pita (pocket) breads

1 In medium bowl, mix mayonnaise, yogurt and seasoned salt. Gently stir in chicken, apple and celery to coat.

2 Cut slit in side of each pita bread to open and form pocket. Fill each with ⅓ cup chicken mixture. Wrap each sandwich securely with foil or plastic wrap; take with you for an on-the-go dinner.

1 Sandwich: Calories 230 (Calories from Fat 70); Total Fat 8g (Saturated Fat 1.5g; Trans Fat 0g); Cholesterol 20mg; Sodium 330mg; Total Carbohydrate 28g (Dietary Fiber 4g) **% Daily Value:** Vitamin A 0%; Vitamin C 0%; Calcium 2%; Iron 10% **Exchanges:** 1½ Starch, ½ Other Carbohydrate, 1 Very Lean Meat, 1 Fat **Carbohydrate Choices:** 2

measuring apples

3 medium apples = 1 pound

1 pound of apples makes 1½ cups of applesauce

1 bushel of apples makes 16 to 20 quarts of juice

A recipe made with mayonnaise and yogurt instead of just mayonnaise will be lower in fat and still have great taste.

Chicken-Bacon-Ranch Wraps

 **Superfast**

Prep Time: 15 Minutes

Start to Finish:
15 Minutes

8 wraps

2½ cups coarsely shredded deli rotisserie chicken (from 2- to 2½-lb chicken)

1 cup shredded Monterey Jack cheese (4 oz)

4 slices cooked bacon, chopped (about ¼ cup)

¼ cup chopped green onions (4 medium)

1 cup fat-free ranch dressing

1 package (11.5 oz) flour tortillas for burritos (8 inch)

4 cups shredded romaine lettuce

1 In large bowl, gently mix all ingredients except tortillas and lettuce. Cover; refrigerate up to 3 days.

2 To make 1 wrap, in small microwavable bowl, microwave generous ⅓ cup chicken mixture, loosely covered, on High 30 to 45 seconds or until hot. Spread chicken mixture on tortilla and top with ½ cup shredded lettuce; roll up.

1 Wrap: Calories 340 (Calories from Fat 120); Total Fat 13g (Saturated Fat 5g; Trans Fat 1g); Cholesterol 55mg; Sodium 910mg; Total Carbohydrate 33g (Dietary Fiber 1g) **% Daily Value:** Vitamin A 30%; Vitamin C 10%; Calcium 20%; Iron 15% **Exchanges:** 1 Starch, 1 Other Carbohydrate, 2½ Medium-Fat Meat **Carbohydrate Choices:** 2

These tasty wraps can also be served cold. For a change of flavor, why not try Cheddar cheese and iceberg lettuce instead of the Monterey Jack and romaine.

Chicken Wraps

Grilled Greek Chicken Sandwiches

Prep Time: 30 Minutes

Start to Finish:
30 Minutes

2 sandwiches

CUCUMBER SAUCE

¼ **cup plain fat-free yogurt**

⅓ **cup finely chopped seeded cucumber**

1 medium green onion, sliced (1 tablespoon)

1 teaspoon grated lemon peel

Salt and pepper to taste

SANDWICHES

2 teaspoons lemon juice

1 teaspoon olive or canola oil

¼ **teaspoon dried oregano leaves**

2 boneless skinless chicken breasts

1 pita (pocket) bread (6 inch), cut in half to form pockets

1 small tomato, sliced

2 thin slices red onion

1 Heat gas or charcoal grill. In small bowl, mix sauce ingredients. Set aside. (Sauce may become watery if it stands longer than 30 minutes.)

2 In another small bowl, mix lemon juice, oil and oregano. Brush lemon mixture over chicken, coating all sides. If desired, sprinkle with salt and pepper.

3 Place chicken on grill over medium heat. Cover grill; cook 15 to 20 minutes, turning once, until juice of chicken is clear when center of thickest part is cut (170°F). Wrap pita halves in foil; place on grill 1 to 2 minutes or until warm.

4 Place chicken, tomato and onion inside pita pockets. Top with sauce.

Alternative Method: Place chicken on broiler pan; broil with tops 4 to 6 inches from heat using times in the recipe as a guide, turning once.

1 Sandwich: Calories 270 (Calories from Fat 60); Total Fat 7g (Saturated Fat 1.5g; Trans Fat 0g); Cholesterol 75mg; Sodium 380mg; Total Carbohydrate 21g (Dietary Fiber 2g) **% Daily Value:** Vitamin A 10%; Vitamin C 20%; Calcium 10%; Iron 10% **Exchanges:** 1 Starch, ½ Other Carbohydrate, 4 Very Lean Meat, ½ Fat **Carbohydrate Choices:** 1½

The creamy cucumber sauce also makes a tasty topper for grilled fish or turkey.

Turkey Caesar Focaccia Wedges ◐ Superfast

Prep Time: 10 Minutes
Start to Finish:
10 Minutes
6 servings

1 package (12 oz) cheese
or garlic focaccia bread
(8 to 10 inch)

3 cups torn romaine lettuce

9 oz cooked turkey, cut into
bite-size strips (2 cups)

⅓ cup reduced-fat creamy
Caesar dressing

¼ cup grated Parmesan
cheese

¼ teaspoon coarse ground
black pepper

1 Cut focaccia bread in half horizontally; set aside.

2 In large bowl, mix remaining ingredients.

3 Spoon turkey mixture evenly onto bottom half of bread.
Cover with top half of bread. Cut into 6 wedges to serve.

1 Serving: Calories 290 (Calories from Fat 90); Total Fat 10g (Saturated Fat 2.5g; Trans Fat 0g); Cholesterol 45mg; Sodium 720mg; Total Carbohydrate 30g (Dietary Fiber 1g) **% Daily Value:** Vitamin A 30%; Vitamin C 10%; Calcium 8%; Iron 15% **Exchanges:** 1½ Starch, ½ Other Carbohydrate, 2 Lean Meat, ½ Fat **Carbohydrate Choices:** 2

Look for the cheese or garlic focaccia bread in the deli
or bakery. Plain focaccia bread or a loaf of soft French
bread can also be used for this sandwich.

Onion-Smothered Barbecued Turkey Burgers

 **Superfast**

See photo, page 122

Prep Time: 20 Minutes

Start to Finish:
20 Minutes

4 sandwiches

1 lb lean (at least 90%) ground turkey

2 tablespoons Italian-style dry bread crumbs

⅓ cup barbecue sauce

1 large sweet or yellow onion

4 whole wheat burger buns or kaiser rolls, split, lightly toasted if desired

1 Set oven control to broil. In medium bowl, mix ground turkey, bread crumbs and half of the barbecue sauce. Shape mixture into 4 patties, ½ inch thick. Place patties on rack in broiler pan.

2 Broil with tops 4 to 6 inches from heat 10 to 12 minutes, turning once, until thermometer inserted in center of patties reads 165°F.

3 Meanwhile, cut onion in half lengthwise; cut crosswise into ¼-inch-thick slices. Separate into half-rings.

4 Heat 10-inch nonstick skillet over medium-high heat. Add onion; cook 2 minutes, stirring frequently. Reduce heat to medium; cover and cook 2 minutes. Stir in remaining barbecue sauce. Reduce heat to medium-low; cover and cook 5 minutes longer or until onion is wilted and sauce thickens.

5 Place patties on bottom halves of buns. Top with onion mixture. Cover with top halves of buns. If desired, serve with additional barbecue sauce.

1 Sandwich: Calories 330 (Calories from Fat 70); Total Fat 8g (Saturated Fat 2g; Trans Fat 0g); Cholesterol 75mg; Sodium 560mg; Total Carbohydrate 32g (Dietary Fiber 4g) **% Daily Value:** Vitamin A 0%; Vitamin C 2%; Calcium 8%; Iron 15% **Exchanges:** 1 Starch, 1 Other Carbohydrate, 4 Very Lean Meat, 1 Fat **Carbohydrate Choices:** 2

Italian Beef Sandwiches

Prep Time: 30 Minutes

Start to Finish:
30 Minutes

4 sandwiches

¾ **lb extra-lean (at least 90%) ground beef**

2 tablespoons unseasoned dry bread crumbs

¼ **cup fat-free (skim) milk**

¾ **teaspoon dried oregano leaves**

½ **teaspoon fennel seed, crushed**

½ **teaspoon garlic powder**

⅛ **to ¼ teaspoon crushed red pepper flakes**

1 medium onion, halved, thinly sliced

1 medium green bell pepper, thinly sliced

1 tablespoon water

4 whole-grain burger buns, split

Mustard, if desired

1 In medium bowl, mix beef, bread crumbs, milk, oregano, fennel, garlic powder and pepper flakes. Shape mixture into 4 patties, ½ inch thick.

2 Heat 8-inch nonstick skillet over medium heat. Add onion, bell pepper and water; cover and cook 5 minutes, stirring occasionally, until vegetables are crisp-tender. Remove vegetables from skillet; cover to keep warm.

3 Wipe skillet clean; heat again over medium heat. Add patties; cook 10 to 12 minutes, turning once, until meat thermometer inserted in center of patties reads 160°F. Serve patties and vegetables in buns. Top with mustard.

1 Sandwich: Calories 270 (Calories from Fat 80); Total Fat 9g (Saturated Fat 3g; Trans Fat 0.5g); Cholesterol 55mg; Sodium 270mg; Total Carbohydrate 25g (Dietary Fiber 4g) **% Daily Value:** Vitamin A 4%; Vitamin C 20%; Calcium 10%; Iron 20% **Exchanges:** 1½ Starch, 2½ Lean Meat **Carbohydrate Choices:** 1½

Try to make small changes. Eat a bit less meat, use skim milk and walk a little more during the day. These small changes will add up over time.

hot off the grill

Swordfish with Pineapple Salsa, see page 165

Beef and Vegetable Packets

Prep Time: 30 Minutes

Start to Finish:
30 Minutes

4 servings

4 medium potatoes, thinly
sliced (4 cups)

8 large mushrooms, sliced
(2 cups)

4 large carrots, thinly sliced
(2 cups)

2 medium onions, sliced

½ lb extra-lean (at least 90%)
ground beef

1 cup barbecue sauce

1 Heat gas or charcoal grill. Cut 4 (20×18-inch) sheets of
heavy-duty foil. Fold each in half to form 10×18-inch
rectangle.

2 In large bowl, mix potatoes, mushrooms, carrots and onions.
Crumble beef over vegetables. Add barbecue sauce; toss until
well coated. Spoon ¼ of mixture onto each sheet of foil. On
each sheet, bring up 2 sides of foil so edges meet. Seal edges,
making tight ½-inch fold; fold again, allowing space for heat
circulation and expansion. Fold other sides to seal.

3 Place packets on grill over medium heat. Cover grill; cook
20 minutes, turning packets over once, until vegetables are
tender and beef is brown. Carefully open packets to allow
steam to escape.

1 Serving: Calories 370 (Calories from Fat 45); Total Fat 5g (Saturated Fat 2g; Trans Fat
0g); Cholesterol 35mg; Sodium 740mg; Total Carbohydrate 65g (Dietary Fiber 7g) **% Daily
Value:** Vitamin A 210%; Vitamin C 25%; Calcium 10%; Iron 30% **Exchanges:** 2 Starch,
1½ Other Carbohydrate, 2 Vegetable, 1 Lean Meat **Carbohydrate Choices:** 4

This is a great all-family meal, and kids love it because
they get their own individual packets.

Grilled Blue Cheese Steak

Prep Time: 30 Minutes

Start to Finish:
30 Minutes

6 servings

2 oz blue cheese, crumbled (½ cup)

1 tablespoon fat-free mayonnaise or salad dressing

1 teaspoon Worcestershire sauce

2 cloves garlic, finely chopped

1½ lb boneless beef sirloin steak, 1½ inches thick

1 Heat gas or charcoal grill. In small bowl, mix cheese, mayonnaise, Worcestershire sauce and garlic until blended; set aside.

2 Place steak on grill over medium-high heat. Cover grill; cook 15 to 20 minutes, turning once, until desired doneness. Remove steak from grill.

3 Spoon cheese mixture over steak; let stand 1 to 2 minutes or until cheese is slightly melted. Cut steak into pieces to serve.

1 Serving: Calories 190 (Calories from Fat 60); Total Fat 7g (Saturated Fat 3g; Trans Fat 0g); Cholesterol 80mg; Sodium 200mg; Total Carbohydrate 1g (Dietary Fiber 0g) **% Daily Value:** Vitamin A 0%; Vitamin C 0%; Calcium 6%; Iron 15% **Exchanges:** 4 Very Lean Meat, 1 Fat **Carbohydrate Choices:** 0

garlic from mild to potent

Garlic has multiple personalities that you can tame through preparation. Hottest and most potent when raw, garlic mellows with cooking.

- For the strongest flavor, add raw garlic to a finished dish or sauce. The more you chop and mince garlic, the more robust it becomes, so if you appreciate the bite but don't want the burn, use whole or halved cloves; remove them before serving.

- Cooking tames garlic's zest and odor. A quick sauté tempers garlic's punch; a long, slow simmer or bake delivers a sweet and nutty essence. As with raw garlic, the smaller the pieces, the fuller the flavor. Watch your garlic sauté carefully; those little pieces burn easily, turning bitter.

- For the most delicate flavor, cook with whole cloves — unpeeled — and remove before serving.

Steak and Potato Salad

Prep Time: 30 Minutes

Start to Finish:
30 Minutes

4 servings (2 cups each)

½ lb small new red potatoes, halved

⅔ cup fat-free honey Dijon dressing

¾ lb boneless beef sirloin steak, ¾ inch thick

¼ teaspoon salt

¼ teaspoon coarse ground black pepper

4 cups torn romaine lettuce

2 medium tomatoes, cut into thin wedges

½ cup thinly sliced red onion

1 Heat gas or charcoal grill. In 2-quart saucepan, place potatoes and enough water to cover. Heat to boiling. Reduce heat to medium; cook 5 to 8 minutes or just until potatoes are fork-tender.

2 Drain potatoes; place in medium bowl. Gently stir in 2 tablespoons of the dressing to coat. Brush steak with 1 tablespoon of the remaining dressing; sprinkle with salt and pepper.

3 Place steak and potatoes on grill over medium heat. Cover grill; cook 8 to 15 minutes, turning once, until steak is desired doneness and potatoes are golden brown.

4 Arrange lettuce, tomatoes and onion on large serving platter. Cut steak into thin slices; arrange on platter. Top with potatoes. Drizzle salad with remaining dressing. If desired, sprinkle with additional black pepper.

1 Serving: Calories 250 (Calories from Fat 30); Total Fat 3.5g (Saturated Fat 1g; Trans Fat 0g); Cholesterol 55mg; Sodium 640mg; Total Carbohydrate 30g (Dietary Fiber 4g) **% Daily Value:** Vitamin A 70%; Vitamin C 45%; Calcium 4%; Iron 20% **Exchanges:** 2 Starch, 2½ Very Lean Meat **Carbohydrate Choices:** 2

> You didn't think that eating healthy could taste this good!

Chicken-Apple Burgers

Prep Time: 25 Minutes

Start to Finish:
25 Minutes

4 sandwiches

1 medium apple, finely chopped (1 cup)

4 medium green onions, finely chopped (¼ cup)

1¼ teaspoons poultry seasoning

½ teaspoon salt

2 tablespoons apple juice or water

1 lb ground chicken or turkey

4 teaspoons honey mustard

4 whole wheat burger buns, split

4 leaves leaf lettuce

1 Heat gas or charcoal grill. In medium bowl, mix apple, onions, poultry seasoning, salt and apple juice. Add ground chicken; mix well. Shape mixture into 4 patties, about ½ inch thick.

2 When grill is heated, carefully oil grill rack. Place patties on grill over medium heat. Cover grill; cook 14 to 20 minutes or until thermometer inserted in center of patty reads 165°F, turning patties once.

3 Spread honey mustard on bottom halves of buns. Top each with lettuce, chicken patty and top half of bun. If desired, serve with additional honey mustard.

To Broil Patties: Place on oiled broiler pan; broil with tops four to six inches from heat, using times above as a guide, turning once.

1 Sandwich: Calories 250 (Calories from Fat 60); Total Fat 7g (Saturated Fat 2g; Trans Fat 0g); Cholesterol 65mg; Sodium 540mg; Total Carbohydrate 21g (Dietary Fiber 3g) **% Daily Value:** Vitamin A 10%; Vitamin C 4%; Calcium 6%; Iron 10% **Exchanges:** 1 Starch, ½ Other Carbohydrate, 3 Very Lean Meat, 1 Fat **Carbohydrate Choices:** 1½

Planning ahead? Make up the chicken patties early in the day, and stack between pieces of waxed paper. Store in the refrigerator until dinnertime, then grill as directed in the recipe.

Chicken with Caramelized Onion-Berry Spread

Prep Time: 30 Minutes

Start to Finish:
30 Minutes

4 servings

½ cup raspberry spreadable fruit

1½ teaspoons grated gingerroot

1 tablespoon red wine vinegar

1 tablespoon soy sauce

2 teaspoons canola oil

1 medium onion, chopped (½ cup)

4 bone-in or boneless chicken breasts, skin removed

1 Heat gas or charcoal grill. In small bowl, beat raspberry spreadable fruit, gingerroot, vinegar and soy sauce with wire whisk until well blended; set aside.

2 In 10-inch nonstick skillet, heat oil over high heat 1 minute. Add onion; cook and stir 2 minutes. Reduce heat to medium; cook 2 minutes longer or until onion is tender and rich dark brown. Reduce heat to low; stir in raspberry mixture. Cook 1 minute, stirring constantly. Remove from heat; set aside.

3 Place chicken, bone side up, on grill over medium-high heat. Cover grill; cook 15 to 17 minutes, turning frequently, until juice of chicken is clear when thickest part is cut to bone (170°F). Serve chicken with onion-berry spread.

1 Serving: Calories 270 (Calories from Fat 60); Total Fat 6g (Saturated Fat 1.5g; Trans Fat 0g); Cholesterol 75mg; Sodium 300mg; Total Carbohydrate 26g (Dietary Fiber 3g) **% Daily Value:** Vitamin A 0%; Vitamin C 4%; Calcium 4%; Iron 8% **Exchanges:** 1½ Other Carbohydrate, 4 Very Lean Meat, 1 Fat **Carbohydrate Choices:** 2

onion equivalents

1 pound dry onions = 3 large or 4 medium onions

1 large onion = about 1 cup chopped

1 medium onion = about ¾ cup chopped

1 small onion = about ⅓ cup chopped

Santa Fe Grilled Chicken

Prep Time: 30 Minutes

Start to Finish: 30 Minutes

8 servings

8 boneless skinless chicken breasts (about 2 lb)

1 tablespoon canola oil

2 tablespoons taco seasoning mix (from 1.25-oz package)

4 slices (¾ oz each) mozzarella cheese, halved

1 cup chunky-style salsa

1 Heat gas or charcoal grill. Brush both sides of chicken with oil; sprinkle with taco seasoning mix.

2 Place chicken on grill over medium heat. Cover grill; cook 15 to 20 minutes, turning once and topping each chicken breast with half slice of cheese during last minute of cook time, until juice of chicken is clear when center of thickest part is cut (170°F).

3 Serve chicken topped with salsa.

1 Serving: Calories 210 (Calories from Fat 80); Total Fat 9g (Saturated Fat 3g; Trans Fat 0g); Cholesterol 80mg; Sodium 430mg; Total Carbohydrate 4g (Dietary Fiber 0g) **% Daily Value:** Vitamin A 8%; Vitamin C 0%; Calcium 10%; Iron 6% **Exchanges:** 4 Lean Meat **Carbohydrate Choices:** 0

- Enjoy the chicken with a cool citrus salad of sliced oranges, grapefruit sections and avocado slices.

- Vary the flavor of this easy entrée by changing the cheese. Why not try Cheddar or Monterey Jack instead of the mozzarella?

Grilled Dill-Mustard Salmon  Superfast

Prep Time: 20 Minutes
Start to Finish:
20 Minutes
6 servings

1 tablespoon chopped fresh dill

1 tablespoon Dijon mustard

1 tablespoon honey

¼ cup fat-free mayonnaise or salad dressing

1½ lb salmon fillet

Cooking spray

1   Heat gas or charcoal grill. In small bowl, mix dill, mustard and honey. In small bowl, place 2 tablespoons mustard mixture; stir in mayonnaise until well blended. Refrigerate mayonnaise-mustard sauce until serving time. Reserve remaining mustard mixture for brushing on salmon.

2   Spray skin side of salmon with cooking spray. Place salmon, skin side down, on grill over medium heat. Spoon reserved mustard mixture onto salmon, spreading evenly. Cover grill; cook 10 to 15 minutes or until fish flakes easily with fork. Serve mayonnaise-mustard sauce with salmon.

To Broil Salmon: Place skin side up on broiler pan; do not spread with mustard mixture. Broil with top four to six inches from heat, using times above as a guide, turning once halfway through broiling and spreading with mustard mixture.

1 Serving: Calories 160 (Calories from Fat 60); Total Fat 7g (Saturated Fat 2g; Trans Fat 0g); Cholesterol 65mg; Sodium 200mg; Total Carbohydrate 4g (Dietary Fiber 0g) **% Daily Value:** Vitamin A 2%; Vitamin C 0%; Calcium 0%; Iron 4% **Exchanges:** 3 Lean Meat **Carbohydrate Choices:** 0

> It's important to separate the portion of the sauce you will be serving later. This ensures that bacteria from uncooked meat or fish will not contaminate the uncooked serving sauce.

Halibut with Chipotle Butter

Prep Time: 30 Minutes
Start to Finish:
30 Minutes
4 servings

1 tablespoon butter or margarine, softened

1 canned chipotle chile in adobo sauce, chopped

1 teaspoon adobo sauce (from can of chipotle chiles)

1 teaspoon lime juice

2 tablespoons chopped fresh cilantro

1 tablespoon olive oil

1 teaspoon chili powder

½ teaspoon garlic salt

½ teaspoon ground cumin

4 halibut steaks (6 oz each)

1 Heat gas or charcoal grill. In small bowl, mix butter, chile, adobo sauce, lime juice and cilantro. Refrigerate until serving time.

2 In another small bowl, mix oil, chili powder, garlic salt and cumin. Brush both sides of each halibut steak with oil mixture.

3 Place halibut on grill over medium heat. Cover grill; cook 10 to 15 minutes, turning once or twice, until fish flakes easily with fork. Serve halibut topped with butter mixture.

To Broil Halibut Steaks: Place on broiler pan; broil with tops four to six inches from heat, using times in recipe as a guide, turning once or twice.

1 Serving: Calories 190 (Calories from Fat 70); Total Fat 8g (Saturated Fat 2.5g; Trans Fat 0g); Cholesterol 80mg; Sodium 320mg; Total Carbohydrate 1g (Dietary Fiber 0g) **% Daily Value:** Vitamin A 10%; Vitamin C 0%; Calcium 2%; Iron 4% **Exchanges:** 3½ Lean Meat **Carbohydrate Choices:** 0

about cumin

Cumin, an earthy-flavored spice, is a key ingredient in many blends of curry and chili powder and is an important seasoning in Latin American and Indian cooking. Cumin is sold in convenient ground form or as whole seeds, which somewhat resemble caraway seeds. Cumin has a fairly penetrating flavor, so add just a little at a time if you're just starting to use it. Try a sprinkle in bean soups, chili or your favorite recipe for meat loaf or meatballs.

Swordfish with Pineapple Salsa

See photo, page 154

Prep Time: 25 Minutes

Start to Finish:
25 Minutes

6 servings

SALSA

½ **medium fresh pineapple, rind removed, cored and finely chopped**

1 **red bell pepper, seeded, finely chopped**

1 **jalapeño chile, seeded, finely chopped**

1 **clove garlic, finely chopped**

¾ **cup finely chopped red onion**

¼ **cup chopped fresh cilantro**

SWORDFISH

½ **cup pineapple juice**

1 **tablespoon grated lime peel**

2 **tablespoons lime juice**

2 **tablespoons rum, if desired**

1 **tablespoon olive or canola oil**

1 **teaspoon paprika or** ¼ **teaspoon ground red pepper (cayenne)**

2 **lb swordfish steaks, cut into 6 serving-size pieces**

1 In medium bowl, mix salsa ingredients. Cover and refrigerate until serving time or up to 4 days.

2 Heat gas or charcoal grill. In shallow dish, mix pineapple juice, lime peel, lime juice, rum, the oil and paprika. Place swordfish in dish; let stand at room temperature 10 minutes to marinate.

3 Place fish on grill over medium heat. Cover grill; cook 8 to 12 minutes, turning once, until fish flakes easily with fork. Serve fish with salsa.

1 Serving: Calories 240 (Calories from Fat 80); Total Fat 9g (Saturated Fat 2.5g; Trans Fat 0g); Cholesterol 80mg; Sodium 75mg; Total Carbohydrate 12g (Dietary Fiber 2g) **% Daily Value:** Vitamin A 20%; Vitamin C 80%; Calcium 4%; Iron 8% **Exchanges:** 1 Other Carbohydrate, 3½ Lean Meat **Carbohydrate Choices:** 1

If you can't get swordfish, try another firm-textured fish, such as grouper, halibut, shark or tuna.

Quick Fish Tacos

Prep Time: 30 Minutes
Start to Finish:
30 Minutes
5 servings (2 tacos each)

1 lb white fish fillets, such as tilapia or catfish

2 tablespoons 40% less-sodium taco seasoning mix (from 1.25-oz package)

3 tablespoons reduced-fat ranch dressing

4 cups coleslaw mix (from 16-oz bag)

1 small jalapeño chile, seeded, finely chopped

10 corn tortillas (6 inch)

1¼ cups sliced radishes (about 10)

Red pepper sauce to taste, if desired

Tomatillo salsa, if desired

1 Heat gas or charcoal grill. Cut 1 (18×12-inch) sheet of heavy-duty foil; spray with cooking spray. Sprinkle both sides of fish fillets with 2 teaspoons of the seasoning mix. Place fish on center of foil sheet. Bring up 2 sides of foil so edges meet. Seal edges, making tight ½-inch fold; fold again, allowing space for heat circulation and expansion. Fold other sides to seal.

2 Place packet on grill over high heat. Cover grill; cook about 10 minutes, rotating packet ½ turn after 5 minutes, until fish flakes easily with fork. Let cool slightly; cut into bite-size chunks.

3 Meanwhile, in large bowl, mix dressing and remaining 4 teaspoons seasoning mix. Add coleslaw mix and chile; toss to coat. Let stand 10 minutes. Meanwhile, wrap stack of tortillas in sheet of foil; place on coolest part of grill 5 to 10 minutes, turning occasionally, until steaming.

4 To serve, spoon about ¼ cup fish chunks and ¼ cup coleslaw mixture onto each tortilla; top with 2 tablespoons radishes. Fold tortillas around filling. Serve with pepper sauce and tomatillo salsa.

1 Serving: Calories 240 (Calories from Fat 35); Total Fat 4g (Saturated Fat 0.5g; Trans Fat 0g); Cholesterol 50mg; Sodium 410mg; Total Carbohydrate 30g (Dietary Fiber 4g) **% Daily Value:** Vitamin A 40%; Vitamin C 40%; Calcium 10%; Iron 8% **Exchanges:** 1½ Starch, 1½ Vegetable, 2 Very Lean Meat, ½ Fat **Carbohydrate Choices:** 2

When chopping the jalapeño chile, wear gloves to prevent skin irritation from the oils.

To warm tortillas in the microwave, place a stack of tortillas between slightly dampened microwavable paper towels; microwave on High about 45 seconds or until warm.

Grilled Marinated Shrimp

Prep Time: 30 Minutes

Start to Finish:
30 Minutes

4 servings

½ teaspoon grated lime peel

¼ teaspoon ground cumin

¼ teaspoon dried oregano leaves

⅛ teaspoon salt

2 tablespoons olive or canola oil

2 tablespoons lime juice

2 cloves garlic, finely chopped

1 lb uncooked deveined peeled large shrimp

1 Heat gas or charcoal grill. In medium bowl, mix all ingredients except shrimp. Add shrimp; toss to coat. Let stand at room temperature 10 minutes to marinate.

2 Remove shrimp from marinade; thread loosely onto 4 (12- to 14-inch) metal skewers. Reserve marinade.

3 Place skewered shrimp on grill over medium heat. Cover grill. Cook 3 to 7 minutes, turning once and brushing occasionally with reserved marinade, until shrimp turn pink. Discard any remaining marinade.

1 Serving: Calories 110 (Calories from Fat 40); Total Fat 4.5g (Saturated Fat 0.5g; Trans Fat 0g); Cholesterol 160mg; Sodium 220mg; Total Carbohydrate 0g (Dietary Fiber 0g) **% Daily Value:** Vitamin A 4%; Vitamin C 2%; Calcium 4%; Iron 15% **Exchanges:** 2½ Very Lean Meat, ½ Fat **Carbohydrate Choices:** 0

This is a great easy recipe because cleanup is at a minimum.

California Bean Burgers

Prep Time: 30 Minutes

Start to Finish:
30 Minutes

6 sandwiches

2 cans (15.5 or 15 oz each)
red kidney beans, drained,
rinsed

¼ cup Italian-style dry bread
crumbs

1 teaspoon Worcestershire
sauce

2 medium green onions,
chopped (2 tablespoons)

1 egg white

3 tablespoons sesame seed

12 slices sourdough bread

¼ cup guacamole

1 medium carrot, shredded
(¾ cup)

1 Heat gas or charcoal grill. Process beans in food processor, or mash in large bowl with fork until smooth. Add bread crumbs, Worcestershire sauce, onions and egg white; process with on/off pulses, or stir until well mixed.

2 Place sesame seed on plate. With wet hands, shape mixture into 6 flat oval-shaped patties, about ½ inch thick. Coat patties evenly on both sides with seed.

3 Place patties on grill over medium-high heat. Cover grill; cook 12 to 16 minutes, turning once, until patties are lightly browned on both sides and seed is toasted.

4 If desired, just before patties are done, place slices of bread on grill to toast lightly.

5 To serve, spread 1 side of each toasted slice of bread with 1 teaspoon guacamole. Top 6 slices of bread, guacamole side up, with patties. Top each with carrot. Cover with remaining bread slices, guacamole side down.

1 Sandwich: Calories 610 (Calories from Fat 70); Total Fat 7g (Saturated Fat 1.5g; Trans Fat 0g); Cholesterol 0mg; Sodium 990mg; Total Carbohydrate 107g (Dietary Fiber 13g) **% Daily Value:** Vitamin A 50%; Vitamin C 6%; Calcium 10%; Iron 45% **Exchanges:** 5½ Starch, 1½ Other Carbohydrate, 1½ Very Lean Meat, ½ Fat **Carbohydrate Choices:** 7

Asparagus on the Grill

Prep Time: 25 Minutes
Start to Finish: 25 Minutes
6 servings

1½ lb fresh asparagus spears

1 tablespoon olive or canola oil

Salt and pepper to taste

1 Heat gas or charcoal grill.

2 Break off tough ends of asparagus spears. Brush asparagus with oil; sprinkle with salt and pepper. Place on grill or in grill basket (grill "wok") over medium heat. Cover grill; cook 5 minutes. Turn asparagus, or shake basket to turn asparagus; cook 3 to 4 minutes longer or until lightly browned and crisp-tender.

3 Place asparagus on serving platter.

1 Serving: Calories 35 (Calories from Fat 20); Total Fat 2.5g (Saturated Fat 0g; Trans Fat 0g); Cholesterol 0mg; Sodium 0mg; Total Carbohydrate 2g (Dietary Fiber 1g) **% Daily Value:** Vitamin A 10%; Vitamin C 2%; Calcium 0%; Iron 8% **Exchanges:** ½ Vegetable, ½ Fat **Carbohydrate Choices:** 0

choosing and using asparagus

- Choose firm, unwrinkled spears with tight tips; the cut ends should be moist, preferably standing in a tray of water. Asparagus is best eaten right away, but will keep if you wrap it tightly in plastic and refrigerate up to three or four days.

- To prepare asparagus, snap off the tough ends by hand near the bottom of the stalk, at the natural breaking point an inch or two from the bottom. Rinse thoroughly. If the stalks still seem sandy, use a paring knife or peeler to remove the triangular "leaves" below the tip. If the stems are tough, peel the skin off the bottom third or so of the spear.

- One pound of asparagus yields two to three servings. Asparagus is a good source of vitamin C and potassium; four large spears contain about 20 calories.

To bump up the flavor, try using a flavored olive oil.

Make a sauce by melting two tablespoons butter and stirring in chopped, drained roasted red bell peppers from a seven-ounce jar. To serve, microwave the sauce uncovered on High 30 seconds. Stir, then microwave 30 to 45 seconds longer or until hot.

Grilled Southwestern Corn

 **Superfast**

Prep Time: 15 Minutes

Start to Finish:
15 Minutes

4 servings (1 ear each)

4 medium ears fresh sweet corn, husks removed

¼ teaspoon salt

2 teaspoons finely chopped fresh cilantro

1 tablespoon olive or canola oil

¼ teaspoon ground cumin

⅛ teaspoon garlic powder

⅛ teaspoon ground red pepper (cayenne)

1 Heat gas or charcoal grill. Carefully brush grill rack with canola oil. Place corn directly on grill over medium-high heat. Cover grill; cook 8 to 10 minutes, turning occasionally, until lightly browned on all sides.

2 Meanwhile, in small bowl, mix salt and cilantro; set aside.

3 In 8-inch nonstick skillet, mix 1 tablespoon oil and the cumin. Cook over medium heat about 30 seconds, stirring frequently, until fragrant. Stir in garlic powder and red pepper. Brush cumin mixture over hot corn; sprinkle with cilantro-salt mixture.

1 Serving: Calories 160 (Calories from Fat 40); Total Fat 4.5g (Saturated Fat 0.5g; Trans Fat 0g); Cholesterol 0mg; Sodium 160mg; Total Carbohydrate 25g (Dietary Fiber 4g) **% Daily Value:** Vitamin A 6%; Vitamin C 6%; Calcium 0%; Iron 4% **Exchanges:** 1 Starch, ½ Other Carbohydrate, 1 Fat **Carbohydrate Choices:** 1½

Omit the cumin, and use fresh dill weed or basil leaves instead of the cilantro.

Serve the corn right off the cob, or scrape the kernels into a bowl and toss with a cup of cooked black beans and a little salsa.

Grilled Sweet Potatoes with Orange-Ginger Butter

⬭ **Superfast**

Prep Time: 20 Minutes
Start to Finish: 20 Minutes
4 servings

2 medium dark-orange sweet potatoes (8 oz each), peeled, cut in half lengthwise

¼ cup water

1 tablespoon butter or margarine, melted

1 teaspoon grated orange peel

½ teaspoon grated gingerroot

¼ teaspoon salt

1 Heat gas or charcoal grill. In 8- or 9-inch square glass baking dish, place sweet potatoes and water. Cover with plastic wrap, folding back one edge ¼ inch to vent steam. Microwave on High 4 to 6 minutes or just until tender; drain.

2 Meanwhile, in small bowl, mix remaining ingredients; set aside.

3 Place potatoes on grill over medium heat. Cook uncovered 3 to 5 minutes, turning frequently and brushing with butter mixture, until potatoes are tender and lightly browned.

1 Serving: Calories 110 (Calories from Fat 25); Total Fat 3g (Saturated Fat 2g; Trans Fat 0g); Cholesterol 10mg; Sodium 200mg; Total Carbohydrate 20g (Dietary Fiber 3g) **% Daily Value:** Vitamin A 360%; Vitamin C 15%; Calcium 4%; Iron 4% **Exchanges:** ½ Starch, 1 Other Carbohydrate, ½ Fat **Carbohydrate Choices:** 1

- Zapping potatoes in the microwave before grilling is a quick and easy trick that helps decrease the overall grill time.

- Low in calories and fat-free, sweet potatoes are chock-full of nutrients like vitamins E, C and B6, potassium and beta-carotene.

Grilled Asparagus and New Potatoes

Prep Time: 30 Minutes
Start to Finish: 30 Minutes
4 servings

2 tablespoons olive oil

½ teaspoon salt

½ teaspoon lemon-pepper seasoning

6 small red potatoes (about ¾ lb), unpeeled, quartered

1 lb fresh asparagus spears

1 Heat gas or charcoal grill. In large shallow bowl, mix 1 tablespoon of the oil, ¼ teaspoon of the salt and ¼ teaspoon of the lemon-pepper seasoning. Add potatoes; toss to coat. Place in grill basket (grill "wok").

2 Place grill basket on grill over medium heat. Cook 15 minutes, shaking grill basket occasionally to turn and mix potatoes.

3 Meanwhile, break off tough ends of asparagus spears. Place asparagus spears in same shallow bowl. Add remaining tablespoon oil, remaining ¼ teaspoon salt and remaining ¼ teaspoon lemon-pepper seasoning; toss to coat.

4 Add asparagus to potatoes in grill basket. Cook about 10 minutes longer or until potatoes and asparagus are tender, shaking basket occasionally to turn and mix vegetables.

1 Serving: Calories 140 (Calories from Fat 60); Total Fat 7g (Saturated Fat 1g; Trans Fat 0g); Cholesterol 0mg; Sodium 340mg; Total Carbohydrate 18g (Dietary Fiber 3g) **% Daily Value:** Vitamin A 10%; Vitamin C 10%; Calcium 4%; Iron 15% **Exchanges:** 1 Starch, 1½ Fat **Carbohydrate Choices:** 1

Grill baskets make it easy to hold and turn vegetables on the grill, but a sheet of foil with a few holes poked through it also works.

sensational sides

chapter

7

Orange-Glazed Carrots and Sugar Snap Peas, see page 194

Creamy Marinated Potato Salad

Prep Time: 10 Minutes
Start to Finish:
30 Minutes
12 servings (½ cup each)

SALAD

1⅓ lb small red potatoes
(8 to 12 potatoes)

3 tablespoons cider vinegar

½ teaspoon salt

4 hard-cooked eggs

8 medium green onions,
sliced (½ cup)

1 medium stalk celery, sliced
(½ cup)

1 small red bell pepper,
coarsely chopped

DRESSING

¾ cup fat-free mayonnaise or
salad dressing

¼ cup fat-free sour cream

1 teaspoon sugar

2 teaspoons prepared
horseradish

2 teaspoons yellow mustard

¼ teaspoon coarse ground
black pepper

1 In 4-quart saucepan or Dutch oven, place potatoes and enough water to cover. Heat to boiling. Reduce heat to medium; cook about 20 minutes or just until potatoes are fork-tender. Drain potatoes; cool slightly. Cut into 1-inch cubes. Place in large nonmetal bowl. Sprinkle with vinegar and salt; toss to coat.

2 Peel and chop eggs. Add to potatoes with remaining salad ingredients; mix gently.

3 In small bowl, mix dressing ingredients. Pour over salad; mix gently to coat. If desired, garnish with additional sliced green onions.

1 Serving: Calories 90 (Calories from Fat 20); Total Fat 2.5g (Saturated Fat 1g; Trans Fat 0g); Cholesterol 75mg; Sodium 270mg; Total Carbohydrate 13g (Dietary Fiber 2g) **% Daily Value:** Vitamin A 8%; Vitamin C 25%; Calcium 4%; Iron 6% **Exchanges:** 1 Starch, ½ Fat **Carbohydrate Choices:** 1

- Prepare this potato salad a day ahead; cover and refrigerate. Just before serving, moisten with one to two tablespoons milk if dry.

- Sprinkling the warm potatoes with vinegar and salt gives them a marinated quality that adds lots of flavor to this salad. The potatoes are most absorbent when warm.

Oven-Roasted Potatoes and Vegetables

Prep Time: 10 Minutes

Start to Finish:
30 Minutes

6 servings (⅔ cup each)

2½ cups refrigerated cooked
new potato wedges
(from 20-oz bag)

1 medium red bell pepper, cut
into 1-inch pieces

1 small zucchini, cut into
½-inch pieces

4 oz fresh whole mushrooms,
quartered (about 1 cup)

2 teaspoons olive oil

½ teaspoon Italian seasoning

¼ teaspoon garlic salt

1 Heat oven to 450°F. Spray 15×10×1-inch pan with cooking spray. In large bowl, toss all ingredients to coat. Spread evenly in pan.

2 Bake 15 to 20 minutes, stirring once halfway through bake time, until vegetables are tender and lightly browned.

1 Serving: Calories 70 (Calories from Fat 15); Total Fat 1.5g (Saturated Fat 0g; Trans Fat 0g); Cholesterol 0mg; Sodium 115mg; Total Carbohydrate 11g (Dietary Fiber 2g) **% Daily Value:** Vitamin A 15%; Vitamin C 25%; Calcium 0%; Iron 4% **Exchanges:** 1 Starch **Carbohydrate Choices:** 1

Experts recommend consuming three to five servings of vegetables each day. This recipe provides a quick and easy way to help you reach that goal.

Skin-On Mashed Potatoes

Prep Time: 10 Minutes

Start to Finish:
30 Minutes

4 servings (¾ cup each)

3 cups cubed (1 to 1½ inch) unpeeled potatoes (1¼ lb)

½ cup plain low-fat yogurt

¼ cup shredded Swiss or Gruyère cheese (1 oz)

2 tablespoons fat-free (skim) milk

½ teaspoon salt

⅛ teaspoon white or black pepper

2 medium green onions, sliced (2 tablespoons)

1. In 3-quart saucepan, place potatoes and enough water to cover. Heat to boiling. Reduce heat to medium; cover and simmer 15 to 20 minutes or until tender. Drain potatoes.

2. In same saucepan or large bowl, mash hot potatoes. Beat in yogurt, cheese, milk, salt and pepper with electric mixer on low speed until light and fluffy. Stir in onions.

1 Serving: Calories 140 (Calories from Fat 25); Total Fat 2.5g (Saturated Fat 1.5g; Trans Fat 0g); Cholesterol 10mg; Sodium 340mg; Total Carbohydrate 23g (Dietary Fiber 3g) **% Daily Value:** Vitamin A 2%; Vitamin C 10%; Calcium 15%; Iron 10% **Exchanges:** 1½ Starch, ½ Fat **Carbohydrate Choices:** 1½

all about potatoes

Selecting Choose firm, clean potatoes free of breaks in the skin or green spots. If green spots develop, trim just before cooking. Remove any "eyes" or sprouts just before cooking.

Storing Remove store-bought potatoes from plastic bags; trapped moisture can result in rotting. Do not wash potatoes before storing. Store potatoes at 45 to 50°F in a dark, well-ventilated place to keep them fresh for several weeks. Light and refrigeration cause potatoes to turn green and develop a bitter flavor.

Preparing Toss peeled potatoes with a little lemon juice to prevent browning if you're not cooking them immediately. Soaking them in cold water results in nutrient loss.

Mashing Russet potatoes are the favored variety for mashed potatoes. Or try Yukon Gold potatoes for a richer, sweeter flavor and creamy yellow color.

Almond-Parmesan Asparagus

 **Superfast**

Prep Time: 20 Minutes

Start to Finish: 20 Minutes

8 servings

2 tablespoons sliced almonds

2 teaspoons butter or margarine

2 teaspoons all-purpose flour

½ cup fat-free half-and-half

⅛ teaspoon salt

Dash pepper

Dash ground nutmeg, if desired

2 lb fresh asparagus spears

½ cup chopped yellow bell pepper

¼ cup shredded Parmesan cheese (1 oz)

1 In 8-inch skillet, cook almonds over medium-low heat 4 to 6 minutes, stirring frequently, until fragrant and lightly browned. Remove from skillet; set aside.

2 In same skillet, melt butter over medium-low heat. With wire whisk, stir in flour until blended. Stir in half-and-half, salt, pepper and nutmeg. Cook, stirring constantly, until mixture boils. Cook 2 to 3 minutes longer, stirring constantly, until thickened. Remove from heat; cover to keep warm.

3 Break off tough ends of asparagus spears. In 4-quart saucepan or Dutch oven, place asparagus; add ½ cup water. Heat to boiling over medium heat. Cook uncovered 3 to 5 minutes or until asparagus is crisp-tender, adding bell pepper during last minute of cooking; drain.

4 On large serving platter, arrange asparagus and bell pepper. Spoon sauce over top; sprinkle with cheese and almonds.

1 Serving: Calories 60 (Calories from Fat 25); Total Fat 3g (Saturated Fat 1.5g; Trans Fat 0g); Cholesterol 5mg; Sodium 125mg; Total Carbohydrate 5g (Dietary Fiber 1g) **% Daily Value:** Vitamin A 10%; Vitamin C 15%; Calcium 8%; Iron 8% **Exchanges:** 1 Vegetable, ½ Fat **Carbohydrate Choices:** ½

Look for fresh asparagus that is bright green with firm, unopened tips. To trim, snap off the tough ends where they break naturally. If desired, use a vegetable peeler to remove the outer layer of the spears.

Creamy Potatoes and Asparagus

 **Superfast**

Prep Time: 20 Minutes

Start to Finish:
20 Minutes

4 servings (1 ¼ cups each)

½ **cup chicken broth**

1 bag (20 oz) refrigerated cooked new potato wedges

1 envelope (1.25 or 1.8 oz) white sauce mix

¾ **cup fat-free (skim) milk**

1 box (9 oz) frozen asparagus cuts

1 In 3-quart saucepan, heat broth to boiling over medium-high heat. Add potatoes; cook 5 minutes.

2 Meanwhile, in small bowl, stir together white sauce mix and milk.

3 Pour sauce over potatoes. Add asparagus; stir gently to mix. Cover; simmer over low heat 7 minutes, stirring occasionally, until sauce thickens and vegetables are crisp-tender.

1 Serving: Calories 170 (Calories from Fat 20); Total Fat 2.5g (Saturated Fat 1g; Trans Fat 0g); Cholesterol 0mg; Sodium 740mg; Total Carbohydrate 29g (Dietary Fiber 4g) **% Daily Value:** Vitamin A 10%; Vitamin C 15%; Calcium 6%; Iron 6% **Exchanges:** 1 ½ Starch, 1 Vegetable, ½ Fat **Carbohydrate Choices:** 2

Cheesy Broccoli Bake

Prep Time: 10 Minutes

Start to Finish:
30 Minutes

6 servings (½ cup each)

1 cup Kix® cereal

2 teaspoons olive oil

4 cups frozen broccoli florets

1 tablespoon butter or margarine

2 tablespoons all-purpose flour

½ teaspoon salt

½ teaspoon ground mustard

⅛ teaspoon pepper

1½ cups fat-free (skim) milk

½ cup shredded reduced-fat sharp Cheddar cheese (2 oz)

1 Heat oven to 400°F. Place cereal in resealable food-storage plastic bag; seal bag and crush with rolling pin. In small bowl, mix cereal and olive oil; set aside. In 1½-quart casserole, place broccoli; cover and microwave on High 3 minutes. Drain; set aside.

2 Meanwhile, in 2-quart saucepan, heat butter until melted. Stir in flour, salt, mustard and pepper. Cook over low heat, stirring constantly with wire whisk, until smooth and bubbly. Remove from heat. Stir in milk. Heat to boiling, stirring constantly. Boil and stir 1 minute; remove from heat. Stir in cheese until melted. Pour sauce over broccoli in casserole. Sprinkle with cereal mixture.

3 Bake uncovered 18 to 20 minutes or until hot.

1 Serving: Calories 150 (Calories from Fat 60); Total Fat 7g (Saturated Fat 3.5g; Trans Fat 0g); Cholesterol 15mg; Sodium 330mg; Total Carbohydrate 13g (Dietary Fiber 3g) **% Daily Value:** Vitamin A 25%; Vitamin C 30%; Calcium 20%; Iron 10% **Exchanges:** ½ Other Carbohydrate, 1 Vegetable, 1 High-Fat Meat **Carbohydrate Choices:** 1

Broccoli and Red Pepper with Lemon-Horseradish Sauce

Superfast

Prep Time: 10 Minutes

Start to Finish:
10 Minutes

6 servings (¾ cup each)

BROCCOLI

1 bag (1 lb) frozen broccoli spears

1 medium red bell pepper, cut into thin bite-size strips

SAUCE

⅓ cup fat-free sour cream

2 teaspoons lemon juice

2 teaspoons Dijon mustard

½ to 1 teaspoon prepared horseradish

¼ teaspoon salt

1 Cook broccoli as directed on bag, adding bell pepper with broccoli. Drain; place in serving bowl.

2 Meanwhile, in small bowl, mix sauce ingredients until smooth.

3 Pour sauce over vegetables. Serve immediately.

1 Serving: Calories 40 (Calories from Fat 0); Total Fat 0g (Saturated Fat 0g; Trans Fat 0g); Cholesterol 0mg; Sodium 170mg; Total Carbohydrate 7g (Dietary Fiber 2g) **% Daily Value:** Vitamin A 30%; Vitamin C 45%; Calcium 4%; Iron 4% **Exchanges:** 1 ½ Vegetable **Carbohydrate Choices:** ½

Red peppers have a delicious sweet taste and are an excellent source of the antioxidant vitamins A and C.

Simmerin' Squash

Prep Time: 5 Minutes

Start to Finish:
25 Minutes

4 servings

1 large acorn squash (2 lb)

½ cup apple juice

1 tablespoon butter or margarine

¼ teaspoon ground cinnamon

1 Trim ends off squash. Stand squash on end; cut in half. Remove and discard seeds and fibers. Cut each squash half crosswise into ½-inch slices.

2 In 12-inch nonstick skillet, mix apple juice, butter and cinnamon. Add squash; heat to boiling. Reduce heat to low; cover and simmer 10 minutes.

3 Turn squash slices; cover and simmer 5 to 8 minutes longer or until squash is tender.

1 Serving: Calories 140 (Calories from Fat 30); Total Fat 3g (Saturated Fat 2g; Trans Fat 0g); Cholesterol 10mg; Sodium 30mg; Total Carbohydrate 27g (Dietary Fiber 7g) **% Daily Value:** Vitamin A 15%; Vitamin C 15%; Calcium 8%; Iron 10% **Exchanges:** ½ Starch, 1 Other Carbohydrate, ½ Fat **Carbohydrate Choices:** 2

about acorn squash

Acorn squash is identifiable by its sharply ridged, dark green skin, splashed with orange. It is shaped like a very big acorn and its flesh is a pale gold color with a mild, sweet flavor.

- Squash is one of the richest vegetable sources of vitamin A and is a good source of vitamin C and dietary fiber.

- Choose squash that's heavy for its size with a firm shell and no cracks or soft spots.

- At home, store the squash in a cool place (50°F) with good air circulation. Refrigerate only after cutting; wrap and store for up to five days.

Orzo-Barley Pilaf

Prep Time: 5 Minutes

Start to Finish:
25 Minutes

4 servings (¾ cup each)

1 can (14 oz) fat-free chicken broth with 33% less sodium

¼ cup water

½ teaspoon dried thyme leaves

¼ teaspoon salt

1 cup sliced fresh mushrooms (3 oz)

½ cup uncooked orzo or rosamarina pasta (3 oz)

½ cup uncooked quick-cooking barley

2 tablespoons sliced green onions (2 medium)

½ teaspoon grated lemon peel

Pepper to taste, if desired

1 In 2-quart nonstick saucepan, heat broth, water, thyme and salt to boiling. Stir in mushrooms, pasta and barley. Return to boiling.

2 Reduce heat to low; cover and simmer 15 to 18 minutes or until pasta and barley are tender and liquid is absorbed.

3 Stir in onions and lemon peel. Season with pepper.

1 Serving: Calories 190 (Calories from Fat 10); Total Fat 1g (Saturated Fat 0g; Trans Fat 0g); Cholesterol 0mg; Sodium 380mg; Total Carbohydrate 39g (Dietary Fiber 5g) **% Daily Value:** Vitamin A 0%; Vitamin C 0%; Calcium 2%; Iron 10% **Exchanges:** 2 Starch, ½ Other Carbohydrate **Carbohydrate Choices:** 2½

grain guide

Barley The characteristic ovals, used in many hearty soups, come in whole or "pearl" forms or ground into flour. Pearl barley has the hull removed, reducing nutrition but speeding up cooking time.

Bulgur Commonly used in pilafs and salads, bulgur is wheat kernels that have been steamed, dried and crushed

Hominy A type of corn that has been dried and hulled, hominy is available ground as grits, canned or finely ground for masa harina, the principal ingredient of corn tortillas and tamales.

Quinoa (KEEN-wah) Mild flavored and light textured, quinoa is a good source of protein. The Incas used the grain extensively; modern shoppers can find it in larger supermarkets and health food stores. It tends to be pricier than most other grains.

Wild rice Harvested primarily in Minnesota and California, "wild rice" is actually a kind of grass. It costs more than ordinary rice, but can be blended with other rices and even a little bit will impart a nutty flavor to a dish.

Quick-cooking barley provides a convenient way to get more whole grains in your diet.

Quick Black Beans and Rice

 **Superfast**

Prep Time: 10 Minutes
Start to Finish: 20 Minutes
5 servings (1 cup each)

¾ cup water

1 can (14.5 oz) Mexican-style stewed tomatoes, undrained

1 can (15.5 oz) black beans, drained

1 cup uncooked instant brown rice

1 cup frozen whole kernel corn

1 medium jalapeño chile, seeded, finely chopped (1 tablespoon)

1. In 8-inch nonstick skillet, mix all ingredients. Heat to boiling.

2. Reduce heat; cover and simmer 12 to 14 minutes or until almost all liquid is absorbed.

1 Serving: Calories 240 (Calories from Fat 10); Total Fat 1.5g (Saturated Fat 0g; Trans Fat 0g); Cholesterol 0mg; Sodium 530mg; Total Carbohydrate 46g (Dietary Fiber 10g) **% Daily Value:** Vitamin A 6%; Vitamin C 8%; Calcium 8%; Iron 15% **Exchanges:** 2 Starch, 1 Other Carbohydrate, ½ Very Lean Meat **Carbohydrate Choices:** 3

bean-efits

Name your bean and you'll find that it's high in dietary fiber and complex carbohydrates. A one-cup serving of beans has about 200 calories and is an excellent source of protein in a low-fat, low-sodium, cholesterol-free package. Beans provide B vitamins, iron and calcium, too.

Basil–Sugar Snap Peas with Mushrooms

 **Superfast**

Prep Time: 20 Minutes

Start to Finish:
20 Minutes

5 servings (½ cup each)

1 tablespoon olive oil

1 cup sliced fresh mushrooms (3 oz)

1 clove garlic, finely chopped

3 cups frozen sugar snap peas

½ cup halved cherry tomatoes

2 teaspoons chopped fresh or ½ teaspoon dried basil leaves

1 tablespoon grated Parmesan cheese

1 In 2-quart saucepan, heat oil over medium heat. Add mushrooms and garlic; cook 3 to 5 minutes, stirring frequently, until tender. Remove from saucepan; place on plate and cover to keep warm.

2 In same saucepan, heat ⅓ cup water to boiling. Add sugar snap peas; return to boiling. Stir; reduce heat to low. Cover; simmer 3 to 5 minutes or until peas are crisp-tender. Drain; return peas to saucepan.

3 Return mushrooms with garlic to saucepan; stir in tomatoes and basil. Spoon into serving bowl; sprinkle with cheese.

1 Serving: Calories 80 (Calories from Fat 30); Total Fat 3.5g (Saturated Fat 0.5g; Trans Fat 0g); Cholesterol 0mg; Sodium 30mg; Total Carbohydrate 8g (Dietary Fiber 3g) **% Daily Value:** Vitamin A 25%; Vitamin C 15%; Calcium 6%; Iron 10% **Exchanges:** ½ Other Carbohydrate, 1 Vegetable, ½ Fat **Carbohydrate Choices:** ½

Each serving of this colorful side dish supplies three grams of fiber and is a good source of vitamin C.

Orange-Glazed Carrots and Sugar Snap Peas

 **Superfast**

See photo, page 178

Prep Time: 15 Minutes

Start to Finish: 15 Minutes

6 servings (½ cup each)

2 cups ready-to-eat baby-cut carrots

1 cup frozen sugar snap peas

2 tablespoons orange marmalade

¼ teaspoon salt

Dash pepper

1 In 2-quart saucepan, heat 1 cup water to boiling. Add carrots; return to boiling. Reduce heat to low; cover and simmer 8 to 10 minutes or until carrots are tender, adding sugar snap peas during last 5 minutes of cook time. Drain; return to saucepan.

2 Stir in marmalade, salt and pepper. Cook and stir over medium heat until marmalade is melted and vegetables are glazed.

1 Serving: Calories 50 (Calories from Fat 0); Total Fat 0g (Saturated Fat 0g; Trans Fat 0g); Cholesterol 0mg; Sodium 130mg; Total Carbohydrate 10g (Dietary Fiber 2g) **% Daily Value:** Vitamin A 140%; Vitamin C 6%; Calcium 2%; Iron 4% **Exchanges:** ½ Other Carbohydrate, ½ Vegetable **Carbohydrate Choices:** ½

Carrots are a well-known source of vitamin A. Did you know that they are also a good source of fiber?

Spinach and Cabbage Slaw

Prep Time: 10 Minutes

Start to Finish:
25 Minutes

6 servings (½ cup each)

2 cups coleslaw mix (from
16-oz bag)

2 cups torn fresh spinach

½ cup thin bite-size strips red
bell pepper

¼ cup light ranch dressing

¼ teaspoon dried dill weed

1   In large bowl, toss all ingredients.

2   Refrigerate at least 15 minutes before serving to blend
flavors.

1 Serving: Calories 40 (Calories from Fat 15); Total Fat 2g (Saturated Fat 0g; Trans Fat 0g);
Cholesterol 0mg; Sodium 110mg; Total Carbohydrate 5g (Dietary Fiber 1g) **% Daily Value:**
Vitamin A 50%; Vitamin C 45%; Calcium 4%; Iron 4% **Exchanges:** 1 Vegetable, ½ Fat
Carbohydrate Choices: ½

Adding spinach and red pepper boosts the vitamin
content of this salad. Spinach is an excellent source
of vitamin A, vitamin K and folic acid. Red pepper
provides vitamins A and C.

Lime and Mango Coleslaw

 **Superfast**

Prep Time: 10 Minutes

Start to Finish:
10 Minutes

12 servings (½ cup each)

2 containers (6 oz each)
Key lime pie low-fat yogurt

1 tablespoon sugar

2 tablespoons vinegar

½ teaspoon ground cumin

5 cups coleslaw mix (from
16-oz bag)

1 ripe large mango, seed
removed, peeled and chopped
(about 1½ cups)

1 In small bowl, mix yogurt, sugar, vinegar and cumin.

2 In 2-quart serving bowl, place coleslaw mix. Top with mango; spoon yogurt mixture over mango. Serve immediately, or cover tightly and refrigerate up to 8 hours. Before serving, toss salad lightly to mix.

1 Serving: Calories 60 (Calories from Fat 0); Total Fat 0.5g (Saturated Fat 0g; Trans Fat 0g); Cholesterol 0mg; Sodium 25mg; Total Carbohydrate 11g (Dietary Fiber 1g) **% Daily Value:** Vitamin A 25%; Vitamin C 25%; Calcium 6%; Iron 0% **Exchanges:** ½ Other Carbohydrate, 1 Vegetable **Carbohydrate Choices:** 1

Fruited Jicama Salad

 Superfast

Prep Time: 15 Minutes

Start to Finish:
15 Minutes

4 servings (1 cup each)

DRESSING

2 tablespoons fresh lime juice

1 tablespoon honey

2 teaspoons water

½ teaspoon poppy seed

½ teaspoon grated orange peel

SALAD

1 cup julienne (matchstick-cut) jicama (1½×¼×¼ inch)

1 seedless orange, peeled, sectioned

1 medium apple, unpeeled, thinly sliced

1 can (8 oz) pineapple chunks in juice, drained

Lettuce leaves, if desired

1 In jar with tight-fitting lid, shake dressing ingredients well. Set aside.

2 In medium bowl, mix salad ingredients. Pour dressing over salad; toss lightly to coat. Cover and refrigerate until serving time. Serve on lettuce-lined salad plates.

1 Serving: Calories 100 (Calories from Fat 0); Total Fat 0g (Saturated Fat 0g; Trans Fat 0g); Cholesterol 0mg; Sodium 0mg; Total Carbohydrate 24g (Dietary Fiber 4g) **% Daily Value:** Vitamin A 2%; Vitamin C 50%; Calcium 4%; Iron 2% **Exchanges:** 1 Fruit, ½ Other Carbohydrate **Carbohydrate Choices:** 1½

sweet treats

"Tealightful" Fruit, see page 200

"Tealightful" Fruit

 **Superfast**

See photo, page 198

Prep Time: 20 Minutes

Start to Finish:
20 Minutes

14 servings (½ cup each)

1 container (16 oz) fresh strawberries, halved (about 3 cups)

2 cups whole dark sweet cherries or 2 ripe mangoes, peeled, pitted, chopped

1 cup seedless green grapes

1 cup fresh blueberries

¼ cup pomegranate juice or grape juice

1 tablespoon balsamic vinegar

1 tablespoon honey

1 teaspoon instant tea mix

1 In large bowl, mix fruit.

2 In jar with tight-fitting lid, shake juice, vinegar, honey and tea mix until well mixed. Pour over fruit; toss gently to coat. Serve immediately.

1 Serving: Calories 50 (Calories from Fat 0); Total Fat 0g (Saturated Fat 0g; Trans Fat 0g); Cholesterol 0mg; Sodium 0mg; Total Carbohydrate 12g (Dietary Fiber 1g) **% Daily Value:** Vitamin A 0%; Vitamin C 35%; Calcium 0%; Iron 0% **Exchanges:** 1 Fruit **Carbohydrate Choices:** 1

- To make this salad up to two hours ahead, leave the strawberries whole, or hold off on adding the dressing until you're ready to serve it.

- Pomegranate juice can be found in single-serve bottles in delis or beverage machines, or in larger economy-size containers in the juice aisle of the grocery store.

Lime-Ginger Fruit Cup

 **Superfast**

Prep Time: 20 Minutes

Start to Finish:
20 Minutes

8 servings (¾ cup each)

¾ **cup sugar**

1 **tablespoon cornstarch**

¾ **cup water**

1½ **teaspoons grated lime peel**

3 **tablespoons fresh lime juice**

1 **teaspoon grated gingerroot**

4 **medium oranges, peeled, sectioned**

3 **medium bananas, sliced**

1 **cup halved fresh strawberries**

1 **cup seedless green or red grapes, halved**

1 In 1-quart saucepan, mix sugar and cornstarch. Stir in water. Heat to boiling over medium-high heat, stirring constantly. Cook until thickened, stirring constantly. Stir in lime peel, lime juice and gingerroot.

2 In large bowl, mix oranges, bananas, strawberries and grapes. Pour lime mixture over fruit; toss gently. Serve immediately, or cover and refrigerate until serving time.

1 Serving: Calories 180 (Calories from Fat 0); Total Fat 0g (Saturated Fat 0g; Trans Fat 0g); Cholesterol 0mg; Sodium 0mg; Total Carbohydrate 43g (Dietary Fiber 3g) **% Daily Value:** Vitamin A 4%; Vitamin C 90%; Calcium 4%; Iron 0% **Exchanges:** 1 Fruit, 2 Other Carbohydrate **Carbohydrate Choices:** 3

Mascarpone-Filled Fresh Strawberries

 **Superfast**

Prep Time: 20 Minutes

Start to Finish:
20 Minutes

20 servings

1 quart large fresh
strawberries

1 container (8 oz)
mascarpone cheese

3 tablespoons powdered
sugar

1 teaspoon milk

½ teaspoon almond extract

Sliced almonds

1 Trim tops and bottoms of strawberries to level. Using small melon baller, scoop out center of each strawberry.

2 In medium bowl, mix cheese, powdered sugar, milk and extract until smooth. Spoon cheese mixture into small resealable freezer plastic bag or decorating bag fitted with star tip; seal bag. Cut small hole in bottom corner of plastic bag. Squeeze bag to pipe cheese mixture into strawberries; top with almonds.

1 Serving: Calories 60 (Calories from Fat 40); Total Fat 4.5g (Saturated Fat 3g; Trans Fat 0g); Cholesterol 10mg; Sodium 5mg; Total Carbohydrate 5g (Dietary Fiber 0g) **% Daily Value:** Vitamin A 2%; Vitamin C 30%; Calcium 0%; Iron 0% **Exchanges:** ½ Other Carbohydrate, 1 Fat **Carbohydrate Choices:** ½

strawberry facts

- Strawberries are an excellent source of vitamin C. Look for plump strawberries with a natural shine, bright red color and fresh-looking green hull. Ripe berries are red throughout. Avoid berries with white "shoulders" (stem ends) and white centers; they're not fully ripe. Unlike tomatoes, they do not ripen after being picked.

- Strawberries are available most of the year. Peak season is May through September.

- To store strawberries, loosely cover them with plastic wrap and refrigerate for up to two days. Wash just before using.

- Rinse strawberries with the hulls still attached to prevent the water from breaking down the texture and flavor inside the berries.

For a beautiful presentation, serve on a bed of coconut on a pretty platter or tray.

Look for mascarpone in the gourmet cheese section of your grocery store. It's usually found near the deli cheeses. In a pinch, cream cheese can be used instead.

Lemon Mini Tarts

Prep Time: 15 Minutes

Start to Finish:
25 Minutes

16 tarts

1 cup fat-free (skim) milk

1 box (4-serving size) lemon instant pudding and pie filling mix

1 teaspoon grated lemon peel

1 refrigerated pie crust (from 15-oz box), softened as directed on box

Strawberry halves, lemon slices or other fresh fruit

Fresh mint leaves

Powdered sugar, if desired

1 In medium bowl, beat milk and pudding mix 2 minutes with electric mixer at medium speed or 2 to 3 minutes with wire whisk until well blended. Stir in lemon peel. Refrigerate.

2 Heat oven to 450°F. Using rolling pin, roll pie crust to 15-inch diameter. With lightly floured 3-inch round cutter, cut 16 rounds from crust; discard scraps. Fit rounds into 16 (2¾-inch) ungreased muffin cups, pressing in gently. Generously prick crusts with fork. Bake 5 to 7 minutes or until very light golden brown. Remove from pan; cool completely.

3 Spoon lemon filling into tart shells. Garnish with fruit and mint; sprinkle with powdered sugar.

1 Tart: Calories 70 (Calories from Fat 25); Total Fat 2.5g (Saturated Fat 1g; Trans Fat 0g); Cholesterol 0mg; Sodium 135mg; Total Carbohydrate 12g (Dietary Fiber 0g) **% Daily Value:** Vitamin A 0%; Vitamin C 4%; Calcium 2%; Iron 0% **Exchanges:** 1 Other Carbohydrate, ½ Fat **Carbohydrate Choices:** 1

Turn these into banana cream tarts by using banana instant pudding and pie filling mix and sliced bananas.

Bake and freeze the crusts up to three months ahead.

Lemon Fruit Dream

 **Superfast**

Prep Time: 10 Minutes

Start to Finish:
10 Minutes

6 servings (½ cup each)

1 can (11 oz) mandarin orange segments, drained

1 can (8 oz) pineapple chunks in juice, drained

2 bananas, cut in half lengthwise, cut into 1-inch chunks

¼ cup halved maraschino cherries, drained

1 container (6 oz) lemon supreme thick & creamy low-fat yogurt

1 In medium bowl, mix all ingredients.

2 Serve immediately.

1 Serving: Calories 120 (Calories from Fat 5); Total Fat 0.5g (Saturated Fat 0g; Trans Fat 0g); Cholesterol 0mg; Sodium 20mg; Total Carbohydrate 26g (Dietary Fiber 2g) **% Daily Value:** Vitamin A 15%; Vitamin C 35%; Calcium 6%; Iron 0% **Exchanges:** 1 Fruit, 1 Other Carbohydrate **Carbohydrate Choices:** 2

- Creamy lemon yogurt changes fruit into a delicious dessert.

- Mix the fruit several hours ahead of time and refrigerate it. Fold in the yogurt just before serving.

Strawberry-Lime Angel Cake

 **Superfast**

Prep Time: 15 Minutes

Start to Finish:
15 Minutes

4 servings

2 cups sliced strawberries

2 tablespoons packed brown sugar

½ teaspoon grated lime peel

1 tablespoon fresh lime juice

4 slices angel food cake, about 1½ oz each

¼ cup frozen (thawed) reduced-fatwhipped topping

1 In medium bowl, mix strawberries, brown sugar, lime peel and lime juice; toss gently to mix well.

2 Place 1 cake slice on each of 4 serving plates. Spoon ½ cup fruit over each cake slice; top each with 1 tablespoon whipped topping.

1 Serving: Calories 190 (Calories from Fat 10); Total Fat 1g (Saturated Fat 0.5g; Trans Fat 0g); Cholesterol 0mg; Sodium 330mg; Total Carbohydrate 41g (Dietary Fiber 2g) **% Daily Value:** Vitamin A 0%; Vitamin C 80%; Calcium 2%; Iron 6% **Exchanges:** 1 Starch, ½ Fruit, 1½ Other Carbohydrate **Carbohydrate Choices:** 3

Fresh Fruit Orange Fizz

 **Superfast**

Prep Time: 10 Minutes

Start to Finish:
10 Minutes

12 servings (½ cup each)

2 cups cubed cantaloupe

2 cups cubed honeydew melon

1 cup halved fresh strawberries

1 large banana, cut in half lengthwise, sliced

½ cup frozen (thawed) orange juice concentrate

¾ cup orange carbonated beverage, chilled

1 In large bowl, gently mix fruit and orange juice concentrate. Stir in carbonated beverage.

2 Serve in small dessert bowls.

1 Serving: Calories 60 (Calories from Fat 0); Total Fat 0g (Saturated Fat 0g; Trans Fat 0g); Cholesterol 0mg; Sodium 10mg; Total Carbohydrate 15g (Dietary Fiber 1g) **% Daily Value:** Vitamin A 20%; Vitamin C 70%; Calcium 0%; Iron 0% **Exchanges:** 1 Fruit **Carbohydrate Choices:** 1

You can cut up all of the fruit except the banana ahead of time. Add the orange juice and carbonated beverage just before serving.

For a potluck, serve the fruit in small plastic cups. Add a touch of fun by moistening and dipping the rim of each cup in colored sugar.

Rice Pudding

Prep Time: 30 Minutes

Start to Finish:
30 Minutes

7 servings (½ cup each)

¾ **cup uncooked regular long-grain white rice**

⅓ **cup raisins**

3 **tablespoons packed brown sugar**

2 **teaspoons vanilla**

½ **teaspoon ground cinnamon**

4 **cups vanilla soymilk**

1 In 3-quart saucepan, heat all ingredients to boiling over medium heat, stirring occasionally; reduce heat to low.

2 Cook uncovered 20 to 25 minutes, stirring frequently, until rice is tender; remove from heat.

3 Serve warm with additional soymilk, if desired. Cover and refrigerate any remaining pudding.

1 Serving: Calories 180 (Calories from Fat 15); Total Fat 2g (Saturated Fat 0g; Trans Fat 0g); Cholesterol 0mg; Sodium 100mg; Total Carbohydrate 35g (Dietary Fiber 0g) **% Daily Value:** Vitamin A 6%; Vitamin C 0%; Calcium 20%; Iron 8% **Exchanges:** 1½ Starch, 1 Other Carbohydrate **Carbohydrate Choices:** 2

This dairy-free dessert is rich, homey and satisfying!

Espresso Cereal Bars

 **Superfast**

Prep Time: 20 Minutes

Start to Finish:
20 Minutes

12 bars

½ **cup corn syrup**

⅓ **cup packed brown sugar**

2 teaspoons instant espresso coffee granules or instant coffee granules

2 teaspoons boiling water

½ **cup creamy peanut butter**

2 cups Basic 4® cereal

1 cup broken pretzel sticks

1 Butter bottom and sides of 8-inch square pan.

2 In 3-quart saucepan, heat corn syrup and brown sugar to boiling over medium-high heat, stirring constantly. Remove from heat. In small bowl, stir coffee granules into boiling water until dissolved; stir into corn syrup mixture along with peanut butter until smooth. Add cereal and pretzels, stirring until evenly coated.

3 Press evenly in pan. For bars, cut into 4 rows by 3 rows. Store covered.

1 Bar: Calories 190 (Calories from Fat 50); Total Fat 6g (Saturated Fat 1g; Trans Fat 0g); Cholesterol 0mg; Sodium 160mg; Total Carbohydrate 29g (Dietary Fiber 1g) **% Daily Value:** Vitamin A 0%; Vitamin C 0%; Calcium 6%; Iron 8% **Exchanges:** 1 Starch, 1 Other Carbohydrate, 1 Fat **Carbohydrate Choices:** 2

- Try adding one-quarter cup dried cranberries, chopped dried cherries or chopped dried apricots to these bars.

- You can increase or decrease the amount of coffee in these bars based on your personal preference.

Chocolate Espresso Mousse

 **Superfast**

Prep Time: 15 Minutes
Start to Finish:
15 Minutes
6 servings (½ cup each)

2 tablespoons light chocolate soymilk

1 tablespoon instant espresso powder or instant coffee granules or crystals

1 oz semisweet or bittersweet baking chocolate

1 cup light chocolate soymilk

1 box (4-serving size) chocolate instant pudding and pie filling mix

2 cups frozen (thawed) fat-free whipped topping

1 In 1-quart saucepan, stir together 2 tablespoons soymilk, the espresso powder and chocolate. Cook over medium heat, stirring constantly, until chocolate is completely melted and mixture is well blended. Cool slightly.

2 In medium bowl, beat 1 cup soymilk and the pudding mix with electric mixer on medium speed or wire whisk 1 to 2 minutes, or until mixture is well blended and thickened.

3 Stir melted chocolate mixture into pudding mixture. Fold in whipped topping. Spoon into individual dessert dishes; serve immediately, or refrigerate until serving time. Cover and refrigerate any remaining mousse.

1 Serving: Calories 140 (Calories from Fat 20); Total Fat 2.5g (Saturated Fat 1.5g; Trans Fat 0g); Cholesterol 0mg; Sodium 280mg; Total Carbohydrate 28g (Dietary Fiber 1g) **% Daily Value:** Vitamin A 0%; Vitamin C 0%; Calcium 6%; Iron 4% **Exchanges:** 1 Starch, 1 Other Carbohydrate **Carbohydrate Choices:** 2

Be a show-off! Top each serving with additional whipped topping, chocolate shavings and a chocolate-covered coffee bean.

Double-Ginger Snack Mix

Prep Time: 10 Minutes

Start to Finish:
30 Minutes

11 servings (½ cup each)

4 cups Total whole-grain
cereal

⅓ cup sliced almonds

1 tablespoon chopped
crystallized ginger

1 bag (7 oz) dried tropical
three-fruit mix

¼ cup packed brown sugar

½ teaspoon ground ginger

2 tablespoons butter or
margarine

¼ cup coconut

1 Heat oven to 300°F. In large bowl, mix cereal, almonds,
crystallized ginger and dried fruit.

2 In 1-quart saucepan, heat brown sugar, ground ginger and
butter over low heat, stirring occasionally, until butter is
melted; stir in coconut. Pour sugar mixture over cereal
mixture; toss until evenly coated. Spread in ungreased
15×10×1-inch pan.

3 Bake 15 minutes, stirring twice. Cool 5 minutes. Store in
tightly covered container.

1 Serving: Calories 150 (Calories from Fat 25); Total Fat 3g (Saturated Fat 1g; Trans Fat
0g); Cholesterol 0mg; Sodium 115mg; Total Carbohydrate 30g (Dietary Fiber 3g) **% Daily
Value:** Vitamin A 10%; Vitamin C 8%; Calcium 6%; Iron 20% **Exchanges:** ½ Starch, 1½ Other
Carbohydrate, ½ Fat **Carbohydrate Choices:** 2

- Fill a half-dozen snack bags with half-cup amounts
of this snack mix and stash close to the door. It's the
perfect treat to take anywhere!

- Almonds supply omega-3 fatty acids that may help
reduce risk of heart disease. They're loaded with
unsaturated fats, so don't go nuts with your portions.

Crunchy Trail Mix Bars

Prep Time: 20 Minutes

Start to Finish:
30 Minutes

36 bars

4 cups Cheerios® cereal

3 cups trail mix (seeds, nuts and dried fruits)

¼ cup butter or margarine

1 cup packed brown sugar

2 tablespoons all-purpose flour

½ cup light corn syrup

1 Grease 13×9-inch pan with shortening, or spray with cooking spray. In large bowl, mix cereal and trail mix; set aside.

2 In 2-quart saucepan, melt butter over medium heat. Stir in brown sugar, flour and corn syrup. Cook, stirring occasionally, until mixture comes to a full boil. Boil 1 minute, stirring constantly.

3 Pour mixture evenly over cereal mixture; toss to coat. Press mixture in pan. Cool 10 minutes. For bars, cut into 6 rows by 6 rows.

1 Bar: Calories 130 (Calories from Fat 45); Total Fat 5g (Saturated Fat 1.5g; Trans Fat 0g); Cholesterol 0mg; Sodium 65mg; Total Carbohydrate 18g (Dietary Fiber 1g) **% Daily Value:** Vitamin A 0%; Vitamin C 0%; Calcium 2%; Iron 8% **Exchanges:** ½ Starch, ½ Other Carbohydrate, 1 Fat **Carbohydrate Choices:** 1

If you plan to bring these to a gathering, cut them into bars and place on a large plastic or paper plate, then cover with plastic wrap or foil for toting. You won't need to carry the pan home!

helpful nutrition and cooking information

Nutrition Guidelines

We provide nutrition information for each recipe that includes calories, fat, cholesterol, sodium, carbohydrate, fiber and protein. Individual food choices can be based on this information.

Recommended intake for a daily diet of 2,000 calories as set by the Food and Drug Administration

Total Fat	Less than 65g
Saturated Fat	Less than 20g
Cholesterol	Less than 300mg
Sodium	Less than 2,400mg
Total Carbohydrate	300g
Dietary Fiber	25g

Criteria Used for Calculating Nutrition Information

- The first ingredient was used wherever a choice is given (such as ⅓ cup sour cream or plain yogurt).

- The first ingredient amount was used wherever a range is given (such as 3 to 3½–pound cut-up broiler-fryer chicken).

- The first serving number was used wherever a range is given (such as 4 to 6 servings).

- "If desired" ingredients and recipe variations were not included (such as sprinkle with brown sugar, if desired).

- Only the amount of a marinade or frying oil that is estimated to be absorbed by the food during preparation or cooking was calculated.

Ingredients Used in Recipe Testing and Nutrition Calculations

- Ingredients used for testing represent those that the majority of consumers use in their homes: large eggs, 2% milk, 80%-lean ground beef, canned ready-to-use chicken broth and vegetable oil spread containing not less than 65 percent fat.

- Fat-free, low-fat or low-sodium products were not used, unless otherwise indicated.

- Solid vegetable shortening (not butter, margarine, nonstick cooking sprays or vegetable oil spread as they can cause sticking problems) was used to grease pans, unless otherwise indicated.

Equipment Used in Recipe Testing

We use equipment for testing that the majority of consumers use in their homes. If a specific piece of equipment (such as a wire whisk) is necessary for recipe success, it is listed in the recipe.

- Cookware and bakeware without nonstick coatings were used, unless otherwise indicated.

- No dark-colored, black or insulated bakeware was used.

- When a pan is specified in a recipe, a metal pan was used; a baking dish or pie plate means ovenproof glass was used.

- An electric hand mixer was used for mixing only when mixer speeds are specified in the recipe directions. When a mixer speed is not given, a spoon or fork was used.

Cooking Terms Glossary

Beat: Mix ingredients vigorously with spoon, fork, wire whisk, hand beater or electric mixer until smooth and uniform.

Boil: Heat liquid until bubbles rise continuously and break on the surface and steam is given off. For rolling boil, the bubbles form rapidly.

Chop: Cut into coarse or fine irregular pieces with a knife, food chopper, blender or food processor.

Cube: Cut into squares ½ inch or larger.

Dice: Cut into squares smaller than ½ inch.

Grate: Cut into tiny particles using small rough holes of a grater (citrus peel or chocolate).

Grease: Rub the inside surface of a pan with shortening, using pastry brush, piece of waxed paper or paper towel, to prevent food from sticking during baking (as for some casseroles).

Julienne: Cut into thin, matchlike strips, using knife or food processor (vegetables, fruits, meats).

Mix: Combine ingredients in any way that distributes them evenly.

Sauté: Cook foods in hot oil or margarine over medium-high heat with frequent tossing and turning motion.

Shred: Cut into long thin pieces by rubbing food across the holes of a shredder, as for cheese, or by using a knife to slice very thinly, as for cabbage.

Simmer: Cook in liquid just below the boiling point on top of the stove; usually after reducing heat from a boil. Bubbles will rise slowly and break just below the surface.

Stir: Mix ingredients until uniform consistency. Stir once in a while for stirring occasionally, often for stirring frequently and continuously for stirring constantly.

Toss: Tumble ingredients (such as green salad) lightly with a lifting motion, usually to coat evenly or mix with another food.

metric conversion guide

VOLUME

U.S. UNITS	CANADIAN METRIC	AUSTRALIAN METRIC
¼ teaspoon	1 mL	1 ml
½ teaspoon	2 mL	2 ml
1 teaspoon	5 mL	5 ml
1 tablespoon	15 mL	20 ml
¼ cup	50 mL	60 ml
⅓ cup	75 mL	80 ml
½ cup	125 mL	125 ml
⅔ cup	150 mL	170 ml
¾ cup	175 mL	190 ml
1 cup	250 mL	250 ml
1 quart	1 liter	1 liter
1½ quarts	1.5 liters	1.5 liters
2 quarts	2 liters	2 liters
2½ quarts	2.5 liters	2.5 liters
3 quarts	3 liters	3 liters
4 quarts	4 liters	4 liters

MEASUREMENTS

INCHES	CENTIMETERS
1	2.5
2	5.0
3	7.5
4	10.0
5	12.5
6	15.0
7	17.5
8	20.5
9	23.0
10	25.5
11	28.0
12	30.5
13	33.0

WEIGHT

U.S. UNITS	CANADIAN METRIC	AUSTRALIAN METRIC
1 ounce	30 grams	30 grams
2 ounces	55 grams	60 grams
3 ounces	85 grams	90 grams
4 ounces (¼ pound)	115 grams	125 grams
8 ounces (½ pound)	225 grams	225 grams
16 ounces (1 pound)	455 grams	500 grams
1 pound	455 grams	½ kilogram

TEMPERATURES

FAHRENHEIT	CELSIUS
32°	0°
212°	100°
250°	120°
275°	140°
300°	150°
325°	160°
350°	180°
375°	190°
400°	200°
425°	220°
450°	230°
475°	240°
500°	260°

NOTE: The recipes in this cookbook have not been developed or tested using metric measures. When converting recipes to metric, some variations in quality may be noted.

index

Note: Numbers in *italics* indicate photos

Hungry for more?

See what else Pillsbury has to offer.

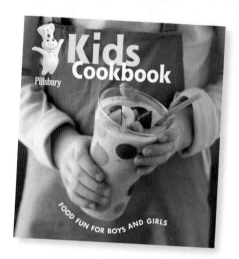

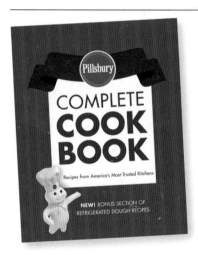